The

Year

of the

Poet VI

November 2019

The Poetry Posse

inner child press, ltd.

The Poetry Posse 2019

Gail Weston Shazor

Shareef Abdur Rasheed

Teresa E. Gallion

hülya n. yılmaz

Kimberly Burnham

Tzemin Ition Tsai

Elizabeth Esguerra Castillo

Jackie Davis Allen

Joe Paire

Caroline 'Ceri' Nazareno

Ashok K. Bhargava

Alicja Maria Kuberska

Swapna Behera

Albert 'Infinite' Carrasco

Eliza Segiet

William S. Peters, Sr.

General Information

The Year of the Poet VI
November 2019 Edition

The Poetry Posse

1ˢᵗ Edition : 2019

Publisher Information
1ˢᵗ Edition : Inner Child Press
intouch@innerchildpress.com
www.innerchildpress.com

ISBN-13 : 978-1-970020-94-6 (inner child press, ltd.)

$ 12.99

WHAT WOULD LIFE BE WITHOUT A LITTLE POETRY?

$\mathcal{D}$edication

This Book is dedicated to

Poetry . . .

The Poetry Posse

past, present & future

our Patrons and Readers

the Spirit of our Everlasting Muse

&

the Power of the Pen

to effectuate change!

In the darkness of my life
I heard the music
I danced . . .
and the Light appeared
and I dance

Janet P. Caldwell

Table of Contents

The Poetry Posse

Table of Contents . . . *continued*

November's Featured Poets 109

Foreword

The definition of Northeast Asia is not static but often changes according to the context in which it is discussed.

In common usage, the term Northeast Asia typically refers to a region including China. In this sense, the core countries constituting Northeast Asia are China, Japan, Taiwan, Mongolia, North Korea and South Korea.

Broader definitions, such as that used by the World Bank refer to the "three major Northeast Asian economies, i.e. China, Japan, South Korea, and Taiwan", as well as Mongolia, North Korea, the Russian Far East and Siberia. The Council on Foreign Relations includes Mongolia and the Russian Far East. The World Bank also acknowledges the roles of sub-national or de facto states, such as Hong Kong and Macau. The Economic Research Institute for Northeast Asia defines the region as "China, Japan, the Koreas, Mongolia, and eastern regions of the Russian Federation".

Despite not being culturally or ethnically East Asian, Russia is sometimes included in discussion as its political interests and policies clashes with those, in particular, of China, Japan, and the Koreas due to its control over the Russian Far East.

The Yellow Sea, the Sea of Okhotsk, and the East China Sea are also included in discussions of the region.

North East Asia is experiencing a large and growing ageing population. The pace of ageing is rapid due to declined fertility and increased longevity, and in some cases shrinking populations. The ageing population with the increasing old-age dependency ratio becomes one of the major challenges to the society, from socio-economic to policy systems. In recent years, North East Asia region is trying to identify technological solutions to assist older adults in independent living and social participation. The assistive technologies also contribute by reducing the burden on their families and caregivers.

The past is haunting Northeast Asia. The China-Japan-Korea triad has been on a repeated collision course over how each perceives the shared past. Bound by dense memory webs, cultural affinity and geographical proximity, each of the three nations has made conflicting historical claims against the other, giving rise to conflict throughout the region and beyond.

China, Japan, and Korea constitute the core of the Northeast Asian "community." "Community" which encompasses "religion, work, family, and culture; it refers to social bonds characterized by emotional cohesion, depth, continuity, and fullness." No community, however, can be totally unified; indeed, national communities can contain antagonistic elements, and the members of a community are not necessarily content with one another. The community of China, Japan, and Korea, like many a marriage, is charged with intense but coexisting feelings of interdependence and conflict, of love and hate.

From a historical perspective, Greater Chinese culture remains the most important influence in this region. Although this statement will lead to opposition from nationalists in other countries. But the history of the origin and development can't be denied. As far as the author's cognition is concerned, since the Tang Dynasty, even earlier, Chinese culture has been deeply implanted in the hearts of all people in this region, whether in political, religious beliefs or lifestyle.

Dr. Tzemin Ition Tsai

World Healing, World Peace Foundation
human beings for humanity

worldhealingworldpeacefoundation.org

World Healing, World Peace 2020
International Poetry Symposium

Dear Friends & Family . . . Poets, Poetry Lovers & Humanitarians

We are so excited at ICPI, Inner Child Press International, as we have begun to mobilize for the upcoming epic event of the 'World Healing, World Peace 2020 Poetry Symposium'. Our plans are set for April of 2020. This event will be held in Atlantic City, New Jersey.

We are now collecting names, emails and telephone numbers for all potential resources that can make this event a highly successful, and one of significance that will have a resounding effect on our world and humanity at large. We are also looking for volunteers who can assist us in many areas of facilitation in the planning, staging and execution phases. Going forward, we will be speaking with the business, government, foundation and the private sectors for funding, sponsorship and suitable venues. So, if you know anything, or know someone, we welcome your input and insights.

We will begin shortly to put together our international guest list.

Communicate with us via our email at :

worldhealingworldpeace@gmail.com

or

whwpfoundation@gmail.com

Visit the Web Site(s) :

worldhealingworldpeacepoetry.com

worldhealingworldpeacefoundation.org

World Healing, World Peace 2020 Anthology is now open for submissions.

Submit to :

worldhealingworldpeace@gmail.com

Please share this information

Thank You

Inner Child Press International
'building bridges of cultural understanding'

www.innerchildpress.com

Preface

Dear Family and Friends,

Yes I am excited? This year we have aligned our vision with that of UNESCO as it honors and acknowledges a variety of Global Indigenous cultures. We are now completing our sixth year of publication. As are on our way to hitting another milestone . . . year 7. Needless to say, we are elated.

Our initial vision was to just perform at this level for the year of 2014. Since that time we have had the blessed opportunity to include many other wonderful word artists and storytellers in the Poetry Posse from lands, cultures and persuasions all over the world. We have featured hundreds of additional poets, thereby introducing their poetic offerings to our vast global readership.

In keeping with our effort and vision to expand the awareness of poets from all walks by making this offerings accessible, we at Inner Child Press International will continue to make every volume a FREE Download. The books are also available for purchase at the affordable cost of $7.00 per volume.

In the previous years, our monthly themes were Flowers, Birds, Gemstones, Trees and Past Cultures. This year we have elected to continue the Cultural theme. In each month's volume you will have the opportunity to not only read at least one poem themed by our Poetry Posse members about such culture, but we have included a few words about the culture in our prologue. The reasoning behind this is that now our poetry has the opportunity to be educational for not only the reader, but we poets as well. We hope you find the poetic offerings insightful as we use our poetic form to relay to you what we too have learned through our research in making our offering available to you, our readership.

In closing, we would like to thank you for being an integral part of our amazing journey.

Enjoy our amazing featured poets . . . they are amazing!

Building Cultural Bridges of Understanding . . .

Bless Up . . . From the home in our hearts to yours

Bill

The Poetry Posse
Inner Child Press Ineternational

PS

Do Not forget about the World Healing, World Peace Poetry effort.

Available here

www.worldhealingworldpeacepoetry.com

For Free Downloads of Previous Issues of
The Year of the Poet

www.innerchildpress.com/the-year-of-the-poet

poetry is . . .

Northern Asia

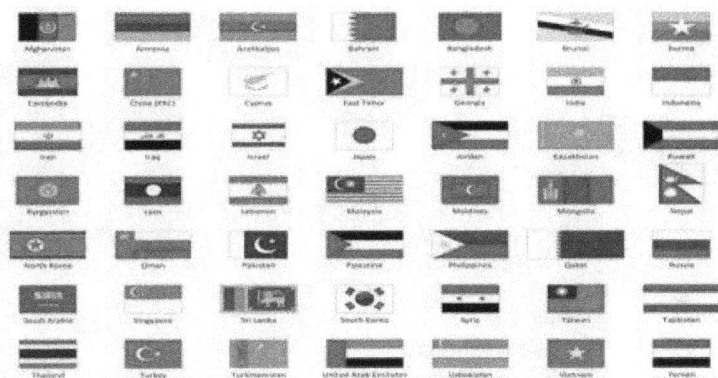

When I searched for some basic information pertaining Northern Asia, I found that most of the information I sought led me to Russia and Eurasia. Through further investigation I was able to obtain information about other countries that should have been included such as Mongolia, China, Japan, North and South Korea, etc. I guess like everything else, information and truth are not always transparent and is rendered to the mercy of he or she who weilds the pen. Below are a couple of web links to help you along the way should you wish to read further about this dynamic and multicultural region of our world.

For more information . . .

https://en.m.wikipedia.org/wiki/Northeast_Asia

https://en.wikipedia.org/wiki/North_Asia

Poets . . .
sowing seeds in the
Conscious Garden of Life,
that those who have yet to come
may enjoy the Flowers.

Poets, Writers . . . know that we are the enchanting magicians that nourishes the seeds of dreams and thoughts . . . it is our words that entice the hearts and minds of others to believe there is something grand about the possibilities that life has to offer and our words tease it forth into action . . . for you are the Poet, the Writer to whom the Gift of Words has been entrusted . . .

~ wsp

Coming
April 2020

Inner Child Press International
!
building bridges of cultural understanding
www.innerchildpress.com

The
World Healing, World Peace
International Poetry Symposium

Stay Tuned

for more information
intouch@innerchildpress.com
'building bridges of cultural understanding'
www.innerchildpress.com

Poetry succeeds where instruction fails.

~ wsp

I FLY

because I Can

...said the Dreamer to the world.

www.iamjustbill.com

Gail Weston Shazor

Gail Weston Shazor

This is a creative promise ~ my pen will speak to and for the world. Enamored with letters and respectful of their power, I have been writing for most of my life. A mother, daughter, sister and grandmother I give what I have been given, greatfilledly.

Author of . . .

"An Overstanding of an Imperfect Love"
&
Notes from the Blue Roof

Lies My Grandfathers Told Me

available at Inner Child Press.

www.facebook.com/gailwestonshazor
www.innerchildpress.com/gail-weston-shazor
navypoet1@gmail.com

North beyond the wall

We have built walls
To fend off the hordes
That would assail us

We have roamed the deserts
Seeking villages
To assimilate
And thus grow our culture

We have considered the nature
Of all things
And how man holds his place
In the evolution of God

We have contemplated
The tones of the Cherry Blossom
And danced within our hearts
With a joyful expectation
Of the coming spring

We have cultivated our crops
In the Paddys filled with water
And upon the sides of the hills . . .
That of our food,
And of our people

We are diverse, yes!
We are many, yes!
We are still . . .
And yet expanding
North beyond the wall

Overstanding

Today I dreamed of the sun
With eyes wide open and looking
Through a window newly clean
Rag in one hand and windex in the other
And just for a moment I could
Smell the ocean wafting
A warm breeze across my feet
So I had to remove my socks
To see if I could wiggle my toes
In a sandy delight of pleasure
I can taste the greenness of
Of your heart holding onto mine
The windowpane seems a doorway
Only I have been asked to enter
When I listen, I can hear your voice
Folding the wings of brown pelicans
And whispering past the lushness
Of the bougainvillea vine
Sweet and sensuous lyrics
Sounding off tamarind clusters
And shooting carambola stars
Calling me to you throughout the day
Upon my prayers gazing beyond glass
I know that you are my overstanding

Love letters…shaped

Of

All the

Things you gave

To me, these I will

Always remember

That you loved me when

When I was unbearable

That you listened always

Without a comment

And that we saw

The moon

Rise

Alicja
Maria
Kuberska

Alicja Maria Kuberska

Alicja Maria Kuberska – awarded Polish poetess, novelist, journalist, editor. She was born in 1960, in Świebodzin, Poland. She now lives in Inowrocław, Poland. In 2011 she published her first volume of poems entitled: "The Glass Reality". Her second volume "Analysis of Feelings", was published in 2012. The third collection "Moments" was published in English in 2014, both in Poland and in the USA. In 2014, she also published the novel - "Virtual roses" and volume of poems "On the border of dream". Next year her volume entitled "Girl in the Mirror" was published in the UK and "Love me" , " (Not)my poem" in the USA. In 2015 she also edited anthology entitled "The Other Side of the Screen".

In 2016 she edited two volumes: "Taste of Love" (USA), "Thief of Dreams" (Poland) and international anthology entitled " Love is like Air" (USA). In 2017 she published volume entitled "View from the window" (Poland). She also edits series of anthologies entitled "Metaphor of Contemporary" (Poland)

Her poems have been published in numerous anthologies and magazines in Poland, the USA, the UK, Albania, Belgium, Chile, Spain, Israel, Canada, India, Italy, Uzbekistan, Czech Republic, South Korea and Australia. She was a featured poet of New Mirage Journal (USA) in the summer of 2011.

Alicja Kuberska is a member of the Polish Writers Associations in Warsaw, Poland and IWA Bogdani, Albania. She is also a member of directors' board of Soflay Literature Foundation.

My Trip to China

I take a long journey to China in my dreams
It's enough for me to find a white cloud in the shape of a
dragon
and I can travel with it through heavenly spaces.
Together, we will bring life-giving raindrops as a gift.

Looking from above, I can see the winding Great Wall,
roofs of temples and water glittering on rice fields.
Our soaring paths are lit by paper lanterns,
hung like colorful dots in the wind.

I admire the meanders of the rivers - Yangtze River and
Huang Ho,
beautiful terraces similar to patchwork bedspreads
 which are covering the majestic Dongchuan Hills,
and Shin Lin formations as gray as the petrified forest

I believe that one day I will go to the Middle Kingdom
I will tie my poems with a red ribbon and go on a journey.
Today I am wearing a jade bracelet,
a symbol of harmony and happiness, the beloved Chinese
stone.

Flower garden

Mother spread a carpet on the fertile ground,
by the damp ribbon of a stream.
Woven of many shapes and colors,
on the canvas of sun's golden rays,
in seeds and rhizomes it stores
the memory of the beauty of past years.

In the morning,
the eyes of flowers moistened by dew,
intensely flash with all colors
like small pieces of stained glass in church windows.
The evening subtly paints the landscape over
with interplay of light and shadow, and adds a shade of
gray.

The garden abides by the laws of nature,
its heart beating to the pace of the seasons.
Both subject to the will of man and independent,
variable in its unbridled beauty,
constantly evades the reign of the creator
– the gardener.

Homeless cat

I observe a homeless cat.
Distrust is hidden in his green eyes,
fear can be seen in the spiked hair
and his paws are always ready to run.

Fate is unkind to him,
it has given the common coat.
People do not admire him
and nobody looks into the cat's soul.

Always hungry and scared,
wandering through the surrounding backyards,
he peeks in the urban garbage.
Sometimes he catches a mouse.

There is no chance of soft pillows,
the abundance of meat and warm milk.
 He does not know the caressing touch of the hand
and the voice of one calling gently- kitty, kitty…

Sometimes he visits the homeless,
They understand each other without words.
The food for a small companion of misery
is waiting in the rusty tin.

Jackie

Davis

Allen

Jackie Davis Allen

Jackie Davis Allen, otherwise known as Jacqueline D. Allen or Jackie Allen, grew up in the Cumberland Mountains of Appalachia. As the next eldest daughter of a coal miner father and a stay at home mother, she was the first in her family to attend and graduate from college. Her siblings, in their own right, are accomplished, though she is the only one, to date, that has discovered the gift of writing.

Graduating from Radford University, with a Bachelors of Science degree in Early Education, she taught in both public and private schools. For over a decade she taught private art classes to children both in her home and at a local Art and Framing Shop where she also sold her original soft sculptured Victorian dolls and original christening gowns.

She resides in northern Virginia with her husband, taking much needed get-aways to their mountain home near the Blue Ridge Mountains, a place that evokes memories of days spent growing up in the Appalachian Mountains.

A lover of hats, she has worn many. Following marriage to her college sweetheart, and as wife, mother, grandmother, teacher, tutor, artist, writer, poet and crafter, she is a lover of art and antiques, surrounding herself, always, with books, seeking to learn more.

In 2015 she authored *Looking for Rainbows, Poetry, Prose and Art*, and in 2017, *Dark Side of the Moon*. Both books of mostly narrative poetry were published by Inner Child Press and were edited by hulya n. yilmaz.

http://www.innerchildpress.com/jackie-davis-allen.php
jackiedavisallen.com

A Moment for all Time

Scenes of design, origin,
A Japanese screen transplanted in kind.
Cherry, gingko, or maple trees;
Some five koi splashed blue.
How beautiful their value's worth.

Painted odd spots of orange.
A winged one, yellow, black, some gold,
Flits and flutters amongst old, spotted blue.
A sun-kissed garden, pink-blushed,
Passionately lush, through and through.

Come lovers of nature.
Peonies for your hats; mossy
Green, for you caps. Consider the blue waters.
Hope for enlightenment, for sweet dreams.
Linger to drink. Linger to think.

Scent of garden's sweet face,
Nature's ancient-brush paints anew
A portrait orientally sublime.
Pen and ink yields a love-linked-scroll;
Poetry finds its way, in moment of time.

Like truth endowed in awe,
Inspired and draped in harmony, hearts race,
Passions pace. And with strange delight....
Catching breath... resting now...
Birds, the swallows, twitter their songs.

Sorry

A pale image, cast by lust, by deceit,
Shame's face is his. He wallows in regret.
The journey, traveled one step at a time.

He questions love, trust. Can they grow anew?

Sipping from tainted glass of decades' past,
He remembers twists and turns. Some sublime.
Stained, he weeps, filled with sorrow and remorse.
Memory. Dreams. He's paralyzed with fear.

Like lessons of history, the world knows
Time immortal awaits closer review.
Pride satisfies neither hunger nor thirst.

O, how his life doth illustrate the years.

Woe, the days of revenge, of betrayal!
They crown his head with weight of shadow's woe.
O, the wounds that strain love's fragile bindings!

Who among you hears his desperate cry?

Mirror of Reflection

From harsh bed of discontent, I rose up.
And, with purpose, took down
From time's creative shelf
The dusty tools, thirsting to be spent.

As I began to sketch a likeness, a portrait
Of myself, I looked deep into the well.

I saw a shadowy reflection staring
Back at me. It was dark with excuses,
With features not unlike those of my own.
Motivated by fear, my past washed clean,

By God's grace I gave thanks
And made note of some plans to better myself.

To improve my lot, I searched
For inspiration. Endowed with pockets
Generously filled with promise,
I invested lavishly.

Never again shall I attempt
To pretend that I am what I am not.

With help in self improvement, I became
A work in progress. I ignored all
The what if's, and with relief,
I buried them in the sand.

Now, the value of my days is measured
By how poetry guides my willing pen.

Tzemin Ition Tsai

Dr. Tzemin Ition Tsai (蔡澤民博士) was born in Republic of China, in 1957. He holds a Ph.D. in Chemical Engineering and two Masters of Science in Applied Mathematics and Chemical Engineering. He is a professor at Asia University (Taiwan), editor of "Reading, Writing and Teaching" academic text. He also writes the long-term columns for Chinese Language Monthly in Taiwan.

He is a scholar with a wide range of expertise, while maintaining a common and positive interest in science, engineering and literature member.

He has won many national literary awards. His literary works have been anthologized and published in books, journals, and newspapers in more than 40 countries and have been translated into more than a dozen languages.

The Night Roar Above The Ancient Dragon Wall

Night secretly hung the moon high again
Light up so many eyes of mine without any extra troubles
Thin twilight looked so sad, like a cat eye blinking in the
    dark
I don't know why
There were always some people go home late at night
Looking for the core of the spirit hidden in the darkness
Been allowed in this city after the nightfall fell
The blackness of darkness reigned
And the perfect stillness was interrupted only by occasional
mutterings of distant thunder
Did not wait until the light of the city out
Insisted that hot wheels must be accurately parked in the
planned position
In the chaotic order
Each seeks to hide
Have not forgotten
How do people love unfettered surprises?
Full of doubts
I really want to know
The rush after mercury spilled all over the floor
How many people will
Directly back to the dream embracing families fall to sleep

The Future And The Past

That completely unfamiliar now
Pull me
Entering the future of the wilderness
The only thing
Could be based on is the impression of walking on the
    fuzzy world
The past is gradually
No longer clear
Can't meet a wise man
Can't stop it
Time does not advance at the same speed
The one that turned back
Suddenly lost a lot of future
The fear of growth is unprecedented
as
Entering the past has passed
Maybe another bunch of right and wrong again
Maybe it's a bunch of futures that are going to past
Maybe
Lying too deep in heart
Or any faint traces will not stay

Why Is The Telephone Getting Dumb?

The pair of big ears lay straight there
Not moving at all
Not making a sound
How long does it?

In the blink of an eye, seven winters quietly slipped past
How to compare with that surges of suffering in my dream
Inadvertently found
It has been covered with gray dust
Catching up with my running dry of emotion pool
By slightly tipsy, I pretended not to remember the ringing
tone in my memory
How is it now ringing in my mind again and again?
Ring, Ring, Ring, Ring …

"Let me be drunk and never wake up!"
Begging myself in my heart
I beg for myself
Even hard to cover my ears is useless
If I can't hold my fingers which always like to tease
And still want to secretly tease the dial buttons again
Yes, no matter inadvertently or
intentionally

Shareef Abdur Rasheed

Shareef Abdur Rasheed

Shareef Abdur-Rasheed, AKA Zakir Flo was born and raised in Brooklyn, New York. His education includes Brooklyn College, Suffolk County Community College and Makkah, Saudi Arabia. He is a Veteran of the Viet Nam era, where in 1969 he reverted to his now reverently embraced Islamic Faith. He is very active in the Islamic community and beyond with his teachings, activism and his humanity.

Shareef's spiritual expression comes through the persona of "Zakir Flo" . Zakir is Arabic for "To remind". Never silent, Shareef Abdur-Rasheed is always dropping science, love, consciousness and signs of the time in rhyme.

Shareef is the Patriarch of the Abdur-Rasheed Family with 9 Children (6 Sons and 3 Daughters) and 41 Grandchildren (24 Boys and 17 Girls).

For more information about Shareef, visit his personal FaceBook Page at :

https://www.facebook.com/shareef.abdurrasheed1
https://zakirflo.wordpress.com

Can't Ignore
----

massive Asia
unparalleled
Asia 30%
earths land mass
60% earths population
bounded by Arctic Ocean
to the north, Pacific
to the east, indian to
the south, Red sea,
inland waters of the Atlantic
Mediterranean and Black sea
to the southwest and on and on
stretches more than 17 million sq.
miles
diversity is a understatement
in it's people's, languages,
climates
the highest point, the lowest
Asia is off the charts
the myriad of contributions
to all mankind in a variety of
sciences
medicine, architecture,
engineering, art, etc.
Asia fast forward
China 2 million Urgar Muslims
in concentration camps,
genocide: Rohingya Muslims
Muslims in Myanmar formally Burma
Muslims in Philippines, Mindanao
targeted
Population of Hong Kong

rises up against violation of
human rights by mainland China
Asia your a monster
all the elements that constitute
mankind
you name it , it's in Asia
you can't ignore her
just try to ignore over 4 Billion
people, 60% of the earths
population

food4thought = education

Handcuffed!
----

by their own foolish,
bull#@!+
stupid laws, rules, policies
so the nation is sinking into
a has been, used to be
wannabe, never mind
used to be, wanna be
never was in the first place
actually
the fact is their laws, rules,
policies often corrupt so
as to maintain status quo
just as long as $$$$'s flow
even though the god dem
trust is dough
it's right on the $#!+ yo!
dem letting you know
this whole joint belongs
to their god shaitan, lucifer
evil personified from the land
that was robbed then soaked
in blood from people
it loved who these folk
made a memory
kidnapped folk to work it
for free
Africans forced into slavery
fast forward today dem still
the predator and people of color,
poor folk, remain yoked
still until today the prey
this whole evil mf'ing joint

is built from forbidden fruit
evil from the root
designed to be 100 proof
poison is the name
from foundation to roof
racing to it's destiny
hell's fire that rage,
black flame!!
tailor made
for the land of murderer's,
thieves
home of the slave

food4thought = education

and dem..,
----
walked away
heard footsteps get faint
me now i the earth
beneath ground
there's no one else around
family, friends were there
in another time, place, space
this is a different world now
no hugs, kisses, wind, rain,
sunshine, noise of hustle,
running all day to get paid
now you lay in a grave
now you will be questioned
who is your lord?
who is your prophet?
what was your way of life?
they call it religion in this life
these are the most crucial
questions ever asked of you
and you need to answer
them all correctly
but you can't if you didn't live
to submit, surrender to the will
of he who made you
put your will away and make his
alone yours
this world, life is a blink
THINK, THINK, THINK
you'll be dead a lot longer
then you lived
what preparations have you made
for your abode

where you will reside forever
as opposed to extensive
preparations made
for a stay of very short duration?

food4thought = education

Kimberly Burnham

Find yourself in the pattern. As a 28-year-old photographer, Kimberly Burnham appreciated beauty. Then an ophthalmologist diagnosed her with a genetic eye condition saying, "Consider life, if you become blind." She discovered a healing path with insight, magnificence, and vision. Today, 33 years later, a poet and neurosciences expert with a PhD in Integrative Medicine, Kimberly's life mission is to change the global face of brain health. Using health coaching, Reiki, Matrix Energetics, craniosacral therapy, acupressure, and energy medicine, she supports people in their healing from brain, nervous system, and chronic pain issues. As managing editor of Inner Child Magazine, Kimberly's 2019 project is peace, language, and visionary poetry with her recently published book, *Awakenings: Peace Dictionary, Language and the Mind, a Daily Brain Health Program.*

http://www.NerveWhisperer.Solutions
https://www.linkedin.com/in/kimberlyburnham

Easy Does It

Easy there

calm down

you will be okay or not

the world needs you to do your best

calmly in the moment like "otsutori"

a Japanese word for easygoing

so calm it seems like time passes slower

than usual, think of what we can all accomplish

the ways we can help ourselves

and the world

surrounded with a sense of peace

"heiwa" in Japanese

filling time so full of meaning

Abandon in Kurdish

An unfeeling computer translates "abandon"
and I wonder does it feel less painful
in Kurdish
these three words that mean abandon
"berdan" sounds like burden
as if it might be okay to abandon a person
when they are a burden
while two other Kurmancî Kurdish words
"dest jê ber dan" and "dev jê berdan"
speak the pain of being abandoned

If I look up "berdan" it means abandon but also
a synonym for allow, divorce, forsake
leave, quit, relinquish, desert ...
and the rhyme pops in my head
a delicious dark chocolate cake dessert
has two "S" because we always want more
the hot dry desert has only one "S"
we wouldn't want to spend too much time there
so it makes sense that another word for forsake
has only one "S"

There are 11 Kurmancî Kurdish words to translate desert
"aran", "berdan", "berrî", "beyaban" "destjêberdan"
"deşit", "sehra", "çol", "çolistan"
"şepal" and "şorezar"
just foreign sounds until we realize
these are the words of someone's life
and the impact
the human toll words take
or the joy "şahî" and "aştî" peace they give

"Aran" is interesting because while it means desert
I am not sure which one
in Turkish there are two words
"elem" translated afflict, excruciate, pain, passion and
suffering
as if we cause pain and inflame passions when we desert
people
and "sancılanmak" translated act, grip, work
it is a confusing rabbit hole
trying to understand how we abandon people
perhaps we must work harder, grip stronger and act more
honorably

In addition to desert "beyaban" can be translated
quiet place or wasteland
as if we don't know what we will leave in our wake
as we depart, desert or abandon
our friends, our human family, our values

"Destjêberdan" is translated desert
abdication and resignation
as if one should abdicate or resign
before deserting one's allies

"Şepal" can also be translated
lioness and oddly, attractive and lovely
as if when like a lioness fiercely we protect
we see more clearly what is attractive and lovely
about the world around us
and we hear the power of our words and work

Cry Aloud

Linguists like biologist measure the endangered
languages considered safe if 100 years from now
three or four generations from today
children will yell and laugh in these special sounds

Words endangered if not
dying when even today no children's voices ring out
in this native tongue
extinct when the last native speaker dies

Like the language of the Mihaq or Kusunda
once "kings of the forest" translated
the "myahq" or "myahak" of central Nepal
where "gepan" and "kegepa" means language
literally "you cry aloud"

But now there is no one left
to cry aloud who is fluent in this repository of culture
and world view we know not what is lost
because these unique images, emotions
dreams, knowledge and beliefs
are no longer transmitted from one generation
to the next

Elizabeth E. Castillo

Elizabeth Esguerra Castillo

Elizabeth Esguerra Castillo is a multi-awarded and an Internationally-Published Contemporary Author/Poet and a Professional Writer / Creative Writer / Feature Writer / Journalist / Travel Writer from the Philippines. She has 2 published books, "Seasons of Emotions" (UK) and "Inner Reflections of the Muse", (USA). Elizabeth is also a co-author to more than 60 international anthologies in the USA, Canada, UK, Romania, India. She is a Contributing Editor of Inner Child Magazine, USA and an Advisory Board Member of Reflection Magazine, an international literary magazine. She is a member of the American Authors Association (AAA) and PEN International.

Web links:

Facebook Fan Page

https://free.facebook.com/ElizabethEsguerraCastillo

Google Plus

https://plus.google.com/u/0/+ElizabethCastillo

Ainu

Vanishing people-
Lurking behind the shadows
Loyal worshippers of Kamuy, their god,
Adapted the exotic Satsuman Culture
Influenced by the Okhotsk, equally enthralling.

Warrior people of many battles they fought,
The Kosyamain, Syaksyain, Kunasi-Menasi
Oppressed and exploited,
These people remained steadfast
Finding their niche in this world.

Wanderers no more,
As the modern age finally recognized them,
Lost world, a forgotten past
The Ainus,
Brave, resilient, children of god.

In His Eyes

there is pure serenity looking at his mesmerizing eyes
a look of wonder, awe and yearning surprise
my wishful future baby yet unborn, the world unfolds,
in your every captivating, sunshiny smiles
reaches the deepest core of my heart
in his eyes, you can see the crystal clear shadow of peace.

as if by drowning in his stares you will lose your sanity
a look of innocence beyond those falling dewey tears
he is the hope of tomorrow's upcoming years.
I can see ageless beauty mirrored in his soul
Erases all those traces of sadness and burdens you thought
you can't bear
spear him from vile creatures who simply aren't pro-lfe for
they don't care!

The Veil of Enigma

It is said that twin flames meet endless times,
In fragments of memories of different lifetimes
Their souls reincarnate and their paths cross magically
through Destiny.
You're an enigma waiting to happen to me
A lurking shadow in my dream within a dream,
Vividly reminiscing your face as those deep set, sullen eyes
Only have this longing stare for me.
Beyond time and space, this thin veil that envelopes
The mystery behind my long search for you,
Will reveal that no matter how many times my earthly body
dies
My spirit will never cease to find you
Even when I'll be put to the ultimate tests,
The veil of enigma surrounding your existence
Brings an undying thrill to my senses.
No, I will not tire of finding my Beloved
Even if it takes me from one world to another,
There is a distinct sweet echo from the mere sound of your
voice
Leaving this heart helpless in such ways one cannot
fathom,
And the first time my eyes met yours
Feels like lounging in a never-ending story of fantasy
For it is just you who possess this magic that enthralls me;
The only one who ignites this burning flame
To heed the call of the Spirit of a Hundred Names.

Joe
Paire

Joe Paire

Joseph L Paire' aka Joe DaVerbal Minddancer . . .
is a quiet man, born in a time where civil liberties
were a walk on thin ice. He's been a victim of his
own shyness often sidelined in his own quest for
love. He became the observer, charting life's path.
Taking note of the why, people do what they do. His
writings oft times strike a cord with the
dormant strings of the reader. His pen the rosined
bow drawn across the mind. He comes full-frontal
or in the subtlest way, always expressing in a way
that stimulate the senses.

www.facebook.com/joe.minddancer

World Traveler

It's harder to get around now
All these borders with social disorder
Oceans of empty ships, trade? Forget about it
Will I ever get to see Japan?
Will I ever get to the top of the highest point of land?
Man!

Peace through words is a beautiful ideology
Shaking hands carries a stronger apology
Now I'm not very adept in foreign policy
However inept I may be, maybe falls on me

I want to attend China's science fare
Does knowledge of a country's atrocities,
 keep me from going there?
 knowing their people are emotionally equal
what is fair?

Passports and visas to see the wonders of the world
World leaders I want to see your beautiful flags unfurled
Asia is huge and rich in culture
People aren't carrion to be fed on like vultures
Let's share our oceans and seas
Some places have to be visited to see
Are we the people or our party
I want to see where it's made
World travelers let's get started.

West Pack

Some of you may know what that means
So I won't explain it, the thing is
I've never been there or so it seems
Now I've heard stories and read text
Yet, I've never been there
I've ordered food from a restaurant
I've eaten cuisine prepared by a native's aunt
But to put your feet on the soil, that's being there.

Trying to explain in your native tongue
watching them laugh when you say something dumb
Rosetta stoned with laughter
but you can't misinterpret a smile
handmade geisha dolls and jade buddhas
The coolest leather jackets embroidered to suit you
Come go with me, Hell! Take home a bride
Words from a briefing, for the rest of your life

A free cruise on you, experience for service members
they tell the stories that get passed on by listeners
I've never been there but I've been there
I have friends to the end that live there
When I share my pen to opening a view
I ask you, can you see it, I ask you, have you seen it
Have you ever been on a west pack cruise?

Way Up Top

I'm out on a limb with my back against the bark
Tiny talons clutch a small branch chomping on seeds
No one can find me up here, I hear them calling my name
Will my new friend take flight and cause them to stare?
Will I follow and forget I can't fly?

Not I, it's safe here, it's humbling it's an escape
It's an escapade in imagination
I am the hunter; I am the prey who hides beyond reach
"Up here in the atmosphere don't bit mo care"
That's an old saying as I'm swaying
Who says you have to grow from growing old
A nine year old can teach

No branch is out of reach so cling to it
swing through the leaves you'll rake later
taste the sap of natures fly trap, it's primal
it's survival of the fittest, it's survival for the witness
Some want to burn the green horizon
I want to share these trees I climb in
Way up top.

hülya

n.

yılmaz

A retired Liberal Arts professor, hülya n. yılmaz [sic] is Co-Chair and Director of Editing Services at Inner Child Press International, and a literary translator. Her poetry has been published in an excess of sixty anthologies of global endeavors. Two of her poems are permanently installed in *TelePoem Booth*, a nation-wide public art exhibition in the U.S. She has shared her work in Kosovo, Canada, Jordan and Tunisia. hülya has been honored with a 2018 WIN Award of British Colombia, Canada. She is presently working on three poetry books and a short-story collection. hülya finds it vital for everyone to understand a deeper sense of self and writes creatively to attain a comprehensive awareness for and development of our humanity.

hülya n. yılmaz, Ph.D.

Writing Web Site
hulyanyilmaz.com

Editing Web Site
hulyasfreelancing.com

hülya n. yılmaz

A Duet with Xue Tao

Xue Tao:

My soul, conforming to this crescent,
dwindles
and flying, now chases a gathering of skies.
Its fine light form, against the darkness, fills
again
and, from all this world of men, its circle can
be seen.
[Xue Tao, "Moon" in *The Brocade River Collection*]
hülya n. yılmaz:
a gentle wind
lowers itself onto the arid leaf
thirsty for the attar of a new breath
awaiting in patience the first drop
underneath layers of the frozen white

it whispers promises anew
unlocks the box after Pandora leaves

she has been tricked . . .

no ill seeps through this time
the bolt's ice will not be melting yet
in joyous dance unite hope and smiles
dreams and love recover again

Goethe calls out as if for me:

"Muses, help me with art,
To suffer joy's pain!"

58

Ludwig Uhland's painless joy
cuddles me with a kissing breeze:

"Oh fresh scent, oh new sound!
Now, poor heart, fear not!
Now everything, everything must change."

[hülya n. yılmaz, "a gentle wind" in *Aflame, Memoirs in Verse*]

A Duet with Daini no Sanmi

Daini no Sanmi:

At the foot of Mt. Arima
the wind rustles
through bamboo grasses
wavering yet constant—
There will never be a moment
that I forget about you.

[No. 58 in *Ogura Hyakunin Isshu* by Fujiwara no Teika]

hülya n. yılmaz:
. . . overlooked the rating
my fatal mistake

too old indeed for this cliché

alas!
mental age
a mere PG-13 as of yet

apologies galore
self-acceptance
an unknown tongue

a pre-natal giver
compensation for the self
a baneful embryo
beyond the reach of life and death

on the edge of tears for evermore

. . .

no more!

no longer willing to carry
emotional baggage for two
that of the old and the new
rendezvoused thus
the first with its end

. . .

sleeping naked tonight
stripped off of the fabric of my favorite clinging

or the so-called events of the past

the big wall clock across my bed
lightened now as it is disassembled
my cleansed head resting on the big hand
the small hand covering me ever so tenderly

come to me tonight oh sweet embrace
you desperately awaited rate of G

. . .

ah!

[hülya n. yılmaz, "annulment" in *Aflame, Memoirs in Verse*]

A Duet with Zhuo Wenjun

Zhuo Wenjun:
Love should be pure, as white as snow on the mountain,
And as bright as the moon amid the clouds.
I heard of your duplicitous intentions,
So I came to break off our relationship.
Today we drink a cup of wine and bid farewell,
Tomorrow we part ways at the moat.
I walk alone above the imperial moat,
And watch the water flowing eastward.
Cold and sorrowful,
A bride at her wedding should not weep.
I want a man who loves me with single-hearted devotion,
And we will stay together as our hair turns white.
A loving couple should be like the shimmering fish
Wriggling at the end of a bamboo rod.
A man who values loyalty
Is worth more than money can buy.
[Zhuo Wenjun, "Song of White Hair"]
hülya n. yılmaz:
once the aged soul
has undressed to the core
layers of her body-fabric become vain

waiting for an annihilating frost to set in,
the inconsolable void might attain its resolve
fanaticizing that the fangs of lost love
have begun at last to will to eat away
the one punica granatum in decay

one red droplet at a time . . .

[hülya n. yılmaz, "a crying Pomegranate" in *Aflame,
Memoirs in Verse*]

Teresa E. Gallion

Teresa E. Gallion was born in Shreveport, Louisiana and moved to Illinois at the age of 15. She completed her undergraduate training at the University of Illinois Chicago and received her master's degree in Psychology from Bowling Green State University in Ohio. She retired from New Mexico state government in 2012.

She moved to New Mexico in 1987. While writing sporadically for many years, in 1998 she started reading her work in the local Albuquerque poetry community. She has been a featured reader at local coffee houses, bookstores, art galleries, museums, libraries, Outpost Performance Space, the Route 66 Festival in 2001 and the State of Oklahoma's Poetry Festival in Cheyenne, Oklahoma in 2004. She occasionally hosts an open mic.

Teresa's work is published in numerous Journals and anthologies. She has two CDs: *On the Wings of the Wind* and *Poems from Chasing Light*. She has published three books: *Walking Sacred Ground, Contemplation in the High Desert* and *Chasing Light.*

Chasing Light was a finalist in the 2013 New Mexico/Arizona Book Awards.

The surreal high desert landscape and her personal spiritual journey influence the writing of this Albuquerque poet. When she is not writing, she is committed to hiking the enchanted landscapes of New Mexico. You may preview her work at

http://bit.ly/1aIVPNq or *http://bit.ly/13IMLGh*

Land of the Rising Sun

The 4th largest island country in the world
with the most educated population in
the 21st century, grew out of feudalism
ruled by the famous shoguns.   The level of
discipline is still high in modern times.

Japan's highly skilled labor force has
made it renowned for its art, video gaming,
cuisine and a major contributor to science and
technology to name just a few.

The issue of an aging population with a high
life expectancy and low birthrate raises a
critical question about the future of life
in the land of the rising sun.

Sightings

We are hovering here to breathe.
Two souls ride a flood of words
as almost one.

Wildfire flirts around our heads.
Tales make us close our eyes
as our lips bend and bleed
on every word.

Happy highs are folded in a blanket.
We run as horses galloping between
a sheet of ecstasy.

A cheating night shuts out the Zen
sounds on authmn's chill.
A book is held close to the bone
in a warm bed.

I find myself a bit shy like a bird
sometimes alone in dreamland.

Forever Time

She is a wanderer gathering
moments with a camera.
At the byways and crossroads,
She catches moments in time.

She seizes blue skies, radiant light,
gurgling rivers, evergreens, wildflowers
playing in meadows, mountain peaks
and creatures great and small.

She captures landscapes around the planet
that showcase Mother Nature's gallery
in all its beauty and diversity.

A digital touch screen locks an image
in forever time to embrace
with the heart over and over again.

Ashok K. Bhargava

70

Ashok Bhargava is a poet, writer, community activist, public speaker, management consultant and a keen photographer. Based in Vancouver, he has published several collections of his poems: Riding the Tide, Mirror of Dreams, A Kernel of Truth, Skipping Stones, Half Open Door and Lost in the Morning Calm. His poetry has been published in various literary magazines and anthologies.

Ashok is a Poet Laureate and poet ambassador to Japan, Korea and India. He is founder of WIN: Writers International Network Canada. Its main objective is to inspire, encourage, promote and recognize writers of diverse genres, artists and community leaders. He has received many accolades including Nehru Humanitarian Award for his leadership of Writers International Network Canada, Poets without Borders Peace Award for his journeys across the globe to celebrate peace and to create alliances with poets, and Kalidasa Award for creative writings.

Narita

On waking up after a restless night
I find my body has been rearranged.

My imagination floats
on the waves of time
seeking ships ready to sail
and Basho
inhaling southern breeze
laced with wasabi aroma
under a maple tree.

Carelessly we click photos
of the wood-beamed monastery and
nobody seems to care
who was the celebrated Haiku-poet
the sea route to China.

A Bridge Between Two

Sky is a sea of gold
filled with giggles of Kanjari
over a small canal.

Curious to meet her lover
a king of kings
she lost her slipper
the in the muddy waters.

She gazed at obsessed
lover and refused to entertain him
until he built a bridge for her.

He kissed her lips
ordered a bridge for his beloved
quenched his thirsty flesh
and left, never to return

Kanjari is a dancing girl.

Why I want Peace

Every chiseled name here is
a bullet dripping blood
a skinned face
a bruised heart

a quagmire
of raw emotions
a breath of trauma

a life martyred: real but mythicized

What could I do
but lament and bow my head
to a life lost

** this poem was composed after I visited the National War
Memorial on October 2, 2019 - 150th birth anniversary of
Mahatma Gandhi an apostle of non-violence.*

Caroline
'Ceri Naz'
Nazareno

Carolin 'Ceri' Nazareno

Caroline Nazareno-Gabis a.k.a. Ceri Naz, born in Anda, Pangasinan known as a 'poet of peace and friendship', is a multi-awarded poet, journalist, editor, publicist, linguist, educator, and women's advocate.

Graduated cum laude with the degree of Bachelor of Elementary Education, specialized in General Science at Pangasinan State University. Ceri have been a voracious researcher in various arts, science and literature. She volunteered in Richmond Multicultural Concerns Society, TELUS World Science, Vancouver Art Gallery, and Vancouver Aquarium.

She was privileged to be chosen as one of the Directors of Writers Capital International Foundation (WCIF), Member of the Poetry Posse, one of the Board of Directors of Galaktika ATUNIS Magazine based in Albania; the World Poetry Canada and International Director to Philippines; Global Citizen's Initiatives Member, Association for Women's rights in Development (AWID) and Anacbanua. She has been a 4th Placer in World Union of Poets Poetry Prize 2016, Writers International Network-Canada ''Amazing Poet 2015'', The Frang Bardhi Literary Prize 2014 (Albania), the sair-gazeteci or Poet-Journalist Award 2014 (Tuzla, Istanbul, Turkey) and World Poetry Empowered Poet 2013 (Vancouver, Canada).

grain of privilege

we all want to put something on our plates,

to satisfy our hunger; to nourish our beings;

but, some have already put their power over

their plates...blinded with supremacy.

what more do you have on your lockers?

snatched last grains,

stolen identities,

grave misconducts

against the farmers' rights

or worst, the land where we grow the grains

for the people, were already hidden down under

that grave called parsimony.

Father Time and Mother Space

The hourglass has been set.
The golden revelation is the reality.
The moment you lift your head
 from the pillow of dreams,
 is a celebration of miracle.
Victories over pains.
Feel the seconds of breathing.
It depicts change and challenge.
The flush of ticks of a wary clock, is not the end.
It calls for the Time of Rising.
The exquisite blood veins
retell the symphony of rebirth;
treasure each other like there's no tomorrow.
This day teaches us to be significant
 in the lives of others.
Mother Space, keeps the distance.
Measurement is sacred .
Try to distance mind from the heart,
but the interconnectedness is there.
In some way, disconnection is needed
 to be independently whole.
 Mindfulness is a space braided with compassion.
Just like motherhood,
a gentle space closest to her heart is her newborn.
This day reminds,
we are natural spaces to create greatness.
 We become academy of spaces:
live to love, love to learn, learn to give.

Let this be…

let this moment
blossom in peace
with your eternal sunshine
in my soul...

let this moment
wander in peace
with your wings
in every shoulder…

let this moment
live in peace
with your sweetest smile
in every face.

.

Swapna Behera

Swapna Behera is a bilingual contemporary poet, author, translator and editor from Odisha, India .She was a teacher from 1984 to 2015 . Her stories, poems and articles are widely published in National and International journals, and ezines, and are translated into different national and International languages. She has penned four books. She was conferred upon the Prestigious International Poesis Award of Honor at the 2nd Bharat Award for Literature as Jury in 2015, The Enchanting Muse Award in India World Poetree Festival 2017, World Icon of Peace Award in 2017, and the Pentasi B World Fellow Poet in 2017.. She is the recipient of Gold Cross Of Wisdom Award ,the medal for The Best Teachers of the World from World Union of Poets in 2018, and The LIfe time Achievement Award ,The Best Planner Award, The Sahitya Shiromani Award, ATAL BiHARI BAJPAYEE AWARD 2018, Ambassador De Literature Award 2018 .She is the Ambassador of Humanity by Hafrikan Prince Art World Africa 2018 and an official member of World Nation's Writers Union ,Kazakhstan2018. At present she is the manager at Large, Planner and Columnist of The Literati, the administrator of several poetic groups ,the member of the Special Council of Five of World Union of Poets and the Cultural Ambassador of Inner Child Press U.S.

An open letter to Bapuji ......

Dear Bapuji,
Are you a vowel or a consonant
a burning flame or a murmuring stream
your spark that extends from the hearth to the heart
from Dandi to the global map
you are the momentum
the eternal existence

How can you run so fast
for a fistful of salt
your thoughts omnipresent beyond all zones
today, tomorrow and forever
Your feeble voice for Satyagraha strengthens
Champaran indigo farmers
you sat on the round table conference
with all your conviction
your twisted spine so empowered
for the common people
your paramount energy of self esteem
dedicated to all
you are the epitome of the liberal voice
how blissfully you loved nature

you are an open invitation
the reflection of truth
let life write and all livelihood cite
your twisted stick, the support
even today the country needs
today also the spines are bent
today also there is violence on the street
the soul is not yet liberated
steps are slow and timid
today also the martyr is sleeping
under the national flag
somewhere another Malala is shot

Even today conspiracy in the name of religion
the palms are burning to get justice
you are the energy
please come once
here is
an open invitation to you
you are our own Bapu
our family member
just hold my soul .... with your voice ...
all respect from India ......

*Bapuji –Mohandas Karamchand Gandhiji, the father of the
Nation of India is popularly known as Bapu who brought
Independence of India by non violence*

*Dandi –the salt satyagraha march started from Dandi a
place in Gujrat, India) as an act of Nonviolent civil
disobedience movement in colonial India by Gandhi. This
began on 12th March 1930 and ended on April 6th 1930*

*Champaran-a place in Bihar from where the satyagraha
movement started by Indigo farmers
during the British colonial period in 1917*

*Malala –Malala Yousafzai is a Pakistani activist for female
education and the youngest Nobel Peace Prize laureate.*

*Satyagraha; - the Insistence or holding firmly to Satya or
TRUTH*

who are you ..?

who are you;
that descends in the milky way
baptize my existence
from evocation to immersion
illuminates my whole Being
celebrates with noise of the words

who are you...?
you call me from invisible
and vanishes at the wink of the eyes
are you a word, a sentence or a mega period?

who are you ...?
you dazzle in the dew drops
on the grass leaves
write the last breathing of a martyr

who are you?
are you the wick of a dark forbidden lane?
or the thin line between virtue and vice
a lover's Pandora box
or the life-saving drops?

who are you...?
the desire for salvation
or the amulets of illusion
fearless banyan tree
or a stable snail
your footsteps are so familiar
here; there and everywhere

just come once
or else allow me to forget you forever
I am good under my thatched roof
where stars twinkle;
and the moon smiles......

Eyes to alphabets

eyes to alphabets
things seem to be hypnotic
but they are often pathetic
how different they are
underneath either a Gulf Stream or a cold Labrador
a flower seller with colours in the traffic square
but a victim with scratches on her cheeks

Eyes to alphabets
the journey is so dynamic
a baby can solace
fire burns within ....
never underestimate the appeal
 the alphabets' deal
they are high voltage power cells
whether you feel or not ......

Albert
'Infinite'
Carrasco

Albert 'Infinite' Carassco

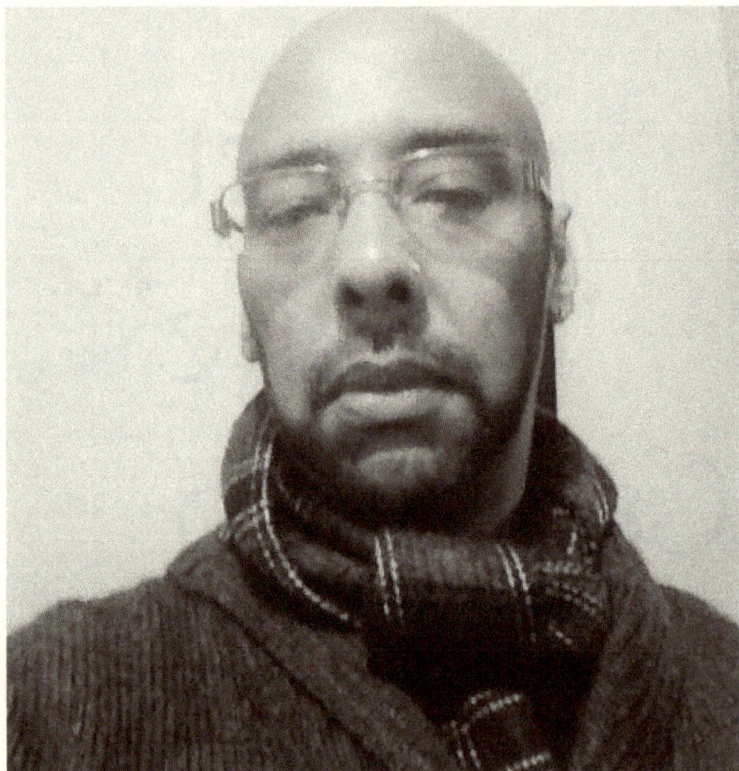

I'm a project life philanthropist, I speak about the non ethical treatment of poor ghetto people. Why? My family was their equal, my great grandmother and great grandfather was poor, my grandmother and grandfather, my mother and father, poverty to my family was a sequel, a traditional Inheritance of the subliminal. I paid attention to the decades of regression, i tried to make change, but when I came to the fork in the road and looked at the signs that read wrong < > right, I chose the left, the wrong direction, because of street life interactions a lot around me met death or incarceration. I failed myself and others. I regret my decisions, I can't reincarnate dead men, but I can give written visions in laymens. I'm back at that fork in the road, instead of it saying wrong or right, I changed it, now it says dead men < > life.

Infinite poetry @lulu.com

Alcarrasco2 on YouTube

Infinite the poet on reverbnation

Infinite Poetry

http://www.lulu.com/us/en/shop/al-infinite-carrasco/infinite-poetry/paperback/product-21040240.html

China

Ancient palaces and temples,
Religious statues,
Vintage dynasty paintings,
T'ai chi Martial arts
Music,
Cultural dance and festivals.
Markets for
Wheat,
rice,
Noodles and vegetables.
Gardens and lakes
Accent beautiful landscapes.
Shanghai Pass to Jiayu Pass
The Great Wall was made for protection,
By rulers of the past.
Clothing isn't just fashion,
Rank and wealth are included,
it's traditional symbolism.
Languages spoken are mostly Cantonese and mandarin,
There's many religions from Buddhism to Judaism.
This is a place definitely on my bucket,
One day I'll travel to China's republic.

Anger issues

Poverty was the start of my anger issues, it's when my father died that i started to act out in irrational ways, my mind was in a daze, i became a youngen caught up in the evil that men do. That's how i was saying dad i miss you. Where his legacy ended I continued, My temper got worse when slugs broke bones and burned through my muscle tissue, that put me on another level, if there's drama I'll shoot first to evade death or laying up in critical, I was on some fuck the world shit, except family and my crew. My team and i lived in the same hood, under similar circumstances, we was on the same page, not having enough filled us with rage, we was bonded but the bond got tighter pushn that white and beige. We was trying to eat, anger would be an understatement explaining the emotions flowing when I saw my kin laid out in the street, on gurneys, in morgues and while standing over their bodies where they'll eternally sleep. One by one the reaper reaped. I went harder and harder after each one returned to the father, I'm a man on fire, I spit flame on the game so mother's don't hear their son expired and to hear "because of your words, I retired", I'm going to save a few, I'm inspired.

Pride and ego

Pride and Egos clash, when they cross paths guns blast, somebody's going to return to ash. Cemeteries are spreading to house the dead and prisons are full of those that fled, the few that went under the radar are a clear and present danger, because after their first, they say it gets easier and easier to eliminate a threat or predators. Out there somewhere there's slugs being loaded into guns for protection and assassination, ya know, defense or habitual 187 offense, out there somewhere someone is living their best life not knowing they're about to die, someone that knows if they get caught it's life and another in shock when they find out they're going to bid forever. Where I'm from it seems as if death is life, I'm used to it, I heard the yells, the cries, the why's, the rum pum pum pum hum of fully and semi automatic murder music. One after the other, over and over another murder, I've lost a lot of brothers, most had no hope,... they didn't get to emergency in an ambulance, they slowly drove off with coroners.

,

Eliza Segiet

Eliza Segioet

After earning a Master's Degree in Philosophy at the Jagiellonian University in Krakaw, Poland, Eliza Segiet proceeded with her post-graduate studies in the fields of Cultural Knowledge, Penal Revenue and Economic Criminal Law, Arts and Literature and Film and Television Production in the Polish city, Lodz.

With specific regard to her creative writings, the author describes herself as being torn in her passion for engaging in two literary genres: Poetry and Drama. A similar dichotomy from within is reflected on Segiet's own words about her true nature: She likes to look at the clouds, but she keeps both of her feet set firmly on the ground.

The author describes her worldview as being in harmony with that of Arthur Schopenhauer: "Ordinary people merely think how they shall 'spend' their time; a man of talent tries to 'use' it".

Brink

Poor millionaires
are like water in a dry river,
broken glass,
leafless trees.

Poor,
childless millionaires
on the verge of life
adopt heirs.

They cross the brink of darkness
in the hope that
Made in Japan will survive.

Before the end they understand
that they are both
rich and beggars,

– they lived to work.

They fulfilled their desires
with the love to work.

Everything else

they postponed
– *for later.*

translated by Artur Komoter

Constellations

He missed out on life.
He forgot that it passes so fast.

He said:
when I was still big
I did not reach for them.

Today I know,
that it will be easier for me to pick mushrooms
than point at the clouds with my finger.

But he also knows
that he can no longer stand up straight.
The time has passed
when he could
watch the constellations of stars.

translated by Artur Komoter

Without a Plan

Life is one,
it is no imitation,
only a harbinger of death.

It will take them all:
ones today,
others tomorrow,
or another time.
It will touch and take away.
Without a plan –
we always go
towards it.

translated by Artur Komoter

William S. Peters Sr.

Bill's writing career spans a period of over 50 years. Being first Published in 1972, Bill has since went on to Author in excess of 40 additional Volumes of Poetry, Short Stories, etc., expressing his thoughts on matters of the Heart, Spirit, Consciousness and Humanity. His primary focus is that of Love, Peace and Understanding!

Bill says . . .

I have always likened Life to that of a Garden. So, for me, Life is simply about the Seeds we Sow and Nourish. All things we "Think and Do", will "Be" Cause and eventually manifest itself to being an "Effect" within our own personal "Existences" and "Experiences" . . . whether it be Fruit, Flowers, Weeds or Barren Landscapes! Bill highly regards the Fruits of his Labor and wishes that everyone would thus go on to plant "Lovely" Seeds on "Good Ground" in their own Gardens of Life!

to connect with Bill, he is all things Inner Child

www.iaminnerchild.com

Personal Web Site

www.iamjustbill.com

Asia North

There have been many,
But none rival the lore
Of the North Asian Dynasties . .

We have the Khans,
The Hahns
The Ming
The Song
Xia . . . 21st - 17th century BC
Shang . . . 17th century BC - 1046 BC
Zhou . . . 1046 - 256 BC
To name a few

There is much to be learned
Much to be given
As we embrace but a taste
Of what there is
Still yet to be discovered,
Uncovered
Instead of obscured
And covered up
By the writers of books
Who assert incomplete looks
At truth

Asia North
Has much to tell . . .
As does the rest of the world
We have so looked down upon . . .
listen

1 eye blind

A deep rose colored monocle
Adorns the left,
The right?

Night endures
Sight obscures
There are no sure- ities
That appease our wonder
Our quest
For truth

The test we face
Has a space ... somewhere
Out there in the nefarious ether,
The never ever neither either
Where you nor I
Can seem to get to

The anguish
Of no light,
Only blight seen
Demeans our essence,
But our very presence
Confirms the present,
Yet to come,
And validates our delusion
Pertaining the illusion s
Of the past
And the future
We must face ...
Can you taste
Your sense of it all

William S. Peters, Sr.

Worry not
About the fall,
For it has already happened
And perhaps ...
We are flapping
Broken wings
Attempting to fly
In the liquid soup
Of subterfugeous dischord

1 eye blind,
The other adorns
A deeply colored
Rose flavored monocle

Smell the flowers my child
Smell the flowers,
For therein lies
The hope you have yet
To grasp.

Poke me in my 3rd eye,
And perchance
I will know you are here
With me

The Saviour is late

Somewhere in the vast darkness
Where light should have been,
The silence was blossoming
As 'Reason' began
To spread its crippled wings

The ignorance was infectious
And a once sacred balance
We species possessed
Had lost it's way

The innate hunger
Of those thirsty for expansion,
For growth,
For clarity,
Now lay upon the roadside
As the blind ones,
The univested wayfarers of life
Numbly,
Rotefully,
Whispered incantations
Unto their own hearts,
Their children,
Seeking to deliberately
Maintain the inauthentic veil
That allowed their
Sleep
To go undisturbed

This is what we have come to,
A quintessential quest-less existence
Where truth had become
A discordant raspy sound,
An annoyance
That aided and abetted

William S. Peters, Sr.

Our dis-ease

Fortunately,
Somewhere in the realm
Of the obscure dreams
Of a few,
There was a light
That was beginning to
Consume their souls
Seeking to purge the despair
And melancholy
That loomed about,
Promising to vanquish the illusion
Of an impending doom ...

But it shall not be,
Nay, it shall not
For the darkness
Can not prophesize
It's own demise
With any certainty,
Without the light

The Saviour is late,
And our fate unfortunately
Is in our own hands.

November

2019

Featured Poets

~ * ~

Rozalia Aleksandrova

Orbindu Ganga

Smruti Ranjan Mohanty

Sofia Skleida

I Fly because I Can

... said the Dreamer to the world.

www.iamjustbill.com

Rozalia Aleksandrova

Rozalia Aleksandrova

Rozalia Aleksandrova lives in Plovdiv, Bulgaria. Author of 11 poetry books: "The House of My Soul" (2000), "Shining Body" (2003), "The Mystery of the Road" (2005), "The Eyes of the Wind" (2007) , "Parable of the key" (2008), "The Conversation between Pigeons" (2010), "Sacral" (2013), "The Real Life of Feelings" (2015), "Pomegranate from Narrow" (2016)... "Everything I did not say"(2019). Editor and compiler of over ten literary almanacs, collections and anthologies. He is a member of the Union of Bulgarian Writers. In 2006 he created a poetic-intellectual association "Quantum and Friends" for the promotion of quantum poetry in civil society, Plovdiv and Bulgarian phenomenon. Initiator and organizer of the International Festival of Poetry "SPIRITUALITY WITHOUT BORDERS".

When Thoughts Draw A Road

When thoughts

draw a road

and shadows pierce the darkness.

A star burns

without flesh.

From the glowing ashes of our fire.

Followed by a meteor shower.

A sunny foal-like sparkle in the eye.

In amazing pure rye

a spark has flickered.

But thoughts draw a road.

And shadows sway.

Love is on its way.

And autumn goes insane.

Promegranate From An Alien

No matter if you love.

Or if you don't.

You are a cry

in the womb

of the Pomegranate.

Splattering

The Time

and Meaning

of the magical grains

for the nectar.

Rozalia Aleksandrova

***

My heart

is a verse,

which is writing

an ode

to you.

Orbindu Ganga

Orbindu Ganga is a post graduate in science and the first recipient of Dr. Mitra Augustine gold medal for academic excellence. He worked in financial, banking and publishing domains. Proved his finesse as a Soft Skills Trainer and Content Account Manager (Client Relationship Manger).

Orbindu Ganga is a multilingual poet, author, critic, content writer, sketch artist, researcher and spiritual healer. His poems have been published in many international publications and anthologies. He has published two research papers in poetry. His painting and article have been published in a spiritual journal - Awakening. He has authored the book "SAUDADE."

Alone in the garden

Smogs were puffing the smoke
Hovering to deny the radiance,
Early misty showers
Wetted the edges of grass,
Tittle of greenery were spread
Opening to the opulence of welkin,
Trying to slice through the fog
A prism of light showered,
Kissing the tip of a grass
A spark of diamond glittered,
Whispering to the shadows around
Garnered many to smile,
A bouquet of fragrance
Smeared in the ambiance,
She was alone
In the open garden,
Smelling the aroma
Heaving with a sigh,
Many smog gathered
To be adsorbed in her,
Never letting any
To be absorbed in her,
Smogs withered
Leaving the lucidity,
Forming a commune
To whisper his thoughts,
Auburn sprinkled butterflies
To see her eyes smiles,
She ricocheted
With a glance,
Gliding in whee
Falling in the stream,
Getting soaked

With his eyes wide open,
Nature rushed with the zephyr
To dry him weather,
He was drenched
Deeply in her thoughts,
Meandering with shadows
Tilting far away,
She had a rare smile
Seeing him fall,
Waited for long
For her smile,
Disappeared before twilight,
Remembering her smile.

Scary Eyes

Dreams have a dream
To fulfil their dreams,
Looking into the firmament
Moving is the clouds,
Slowly in a pace
Known to appraise,
Forming many forms
With a sign to gaze,
Whispering at the forms
Drawing on the sands,
Flying among the clouds
Inundated mind of bliss,
Silence had a thought
To giggle among the lots,
Innocence maneuvered
In the veins of many,
Drafted from the years
With the cultural synergy.

A silent night was blighted
With smokes of terror,
The moon was hidden
In the cusp of strikes,
Lighting of crackers
Brightened the nights,
Cry of innocence was heard
Far away from the lights,
Night was long
With bombed edifices,
Looking for help
Many dusted in silence,
Crevices of pain
Waited for the light,

Old slumbered
Without a voice,
Children were crying
With none to hear.

Auburn opened
Resting was the forms,
Children thawed
To see the bodies around,
Eyes were opened
Never to close,
Rivers were slowly flowing
With eyes never to blink,
Looking in the firmament
With smokes moving,
In a state of denial
Terrified eyes wandered,
None to hold their hands
Fear whispered deep,
Crawling to seek attention
Bodies were dusted in silence,
Scary eyes pleaded
For a hope for life.

Dilapidated Edifice

Down in the downtown
Along the slopes,
Sliding with loops
And meandering curves,
Lived many souls
Away from the crescendo,
A world lesser
Known to many,
Morning dust lighted
With many eyes brightened,
Ambling along
The hair pins,
Listening to the hovering
Singers of nature,
Calling for the onlookers
With a chirpy melody,
Lived an edifice
Living for others,
Life had a line
Encircling the line,
Food and water
Buffering the core,
Grafted with items
For the houses to store,
Getting from far away
Was a journey with a smile,
Being for the people
Travel never tired their minds,
Standing tall against
The mighty time,
Having the blessings
From all around,
A selfless thought triggered

Within the self,
Traveling on a rainy night
Roads opened wider,
Leaving the slopes
To aghast in wander,
Sliding on the curve
Leaving them fall forever,
Tears were flowing
Never to stop,
Years have gone
Weeping in rust,
Standing alone
Dilapidated in tears,
Lifeline showers
Memories of yestreen,
The edifice symbolises
A hope to revive the past.

Orbindu Ganga

Smruti Ranjan Mohanty

Smruti Ranjan Mohanty, son of Raj Kishore and Shantilata Mohanty, born at Padmapur, Jagatsinghpur, Odisha on 1.1.1963 is a multilingual poet, essayist and writer. He is a published poet and writer and a featured poet of PENTASI B World Friendship Poetry. His writings include essays, short stories, poems and novels which are published in newspapers and in various national and international magazines, journals and anthologies. Working as Finance Officer in Govt of Odisha, he writes extensively on life, its beauty and intricacies which are widely acclaimed.

Website
smrutiweb.wordpress.com

The Queen Of Night

oh, the queen of the night!
i will never succumb to your first kiss
you have to come with all your charm
to seduce me, make me fall in love with
you are to knock at me, knock at my closed door,
again and again,
to win me, win my body, mind and heart

I know not how many times i am here
how many times we met and part
but as and when i come
you chase me like a mad beloved
to meet me, feel my touch and feel me deep inside

my love!
we part to meet and meet to part
that define our love and romance
but our joy and ecstasy
only for few moments
then begins the journey of life,
its chill and charm and that long waiting to give meaning
to that eternal love and longing

my love!
waiting for you since long
i know you are behind my back since the day i am here,
come in front, face to face
come with your spellbinding grandeur
i will unveil that veil and
see the girl of my dreams once more

come with your filigree smile
drooping eyes and quivering lips

i could see you, see your body,
its curves speaking volumes of your love and longing
look at me, take me in your hands
let me see how spellbinding my fiancee is

Loyalty

loyalty to what and whom?
to an individual
who does not understand its meaning
to a relationship
that stands on permanent interests and hypocrisy
to an idea
that misguides and takes one to the brink of a calamity
or to something else?

when loyalty makes one blind to the reality
when based on negative reasons and unscientific reasoning,
how hazardous it is, instead of fulfilling, it kills the man
within

in roles and relationships man lives
remaining true and doing justice to one's roles,
individuals, relationships and values in thoughts, words and
deeds
is what define loyalty

it is never a blind commitment to naked self-interests,
dogmas, superstitions and the forces and beliefs,
attitudes and endeavours that is against truth and justice
man and humanity

responding to the larger society
its needs and values, collective conscience
and betterment of humanity
is what mean loyalty
to remain loyal to others
you are to be loyal to yourself
to the man within, to your inner voice
the values you inculcated

the more you are loyal to yourself
the more you are loyal to the rest
to truth, love, peace and brotherhood
when you are true and loyal to your conscience,
you make others loyal and become a better man

people and ideologies will come and go,
relationships are cultivated, institutions grow and decline,
but one's loyalty is beyond these, always to the betterment
of humanity

loyalty to an individual, to an institution, towards an
ideology,
man and his whims and caprices irrespective of the goals
they strive,
means they adopt, which your inner you never accept
is but disloyalty to man and the society
let your loyalty be full and complete
to your love and relationships, ideas and idols
and anything you consider true and genuine

loyalty lies in listening to the voice of humanity,
in a commitment to ideas, endeavours and relationships
that is an integral part of man and his development,
always in tune with decency and morality,
law of the land and betterment of society

I Am In Love

for a change
we just looked at each other
and the rest is history
life unfolded its beauty like never before

we are in love once more
how soon everything changed
and the world became so beautiful and fascinating once
again

i looked at you
you are the same, no signs of ageing, no wrinkles, no black
spots,
i could see nothing, only sense that ageless heart beating
for the sake of love
those beautiful eyes, dancing dimples, rosy cheeks,
quivering lips,
drooping eyes and inviting gestures telling me
it is not all over
still, there is enough in us
to captivate each other for years together

love is always in its youth
love never grows old, it is as it was
much before when we first fell in love
we don't feel it, feel its warmth and beauty
because we never look at it
the way we used to look at it
life is all about finding that love
rediscovering the moments
and passion for each other

life is living gracefully
falling in love with one's love
falling in love with oneself
and life again and again
irrespective of the situation
and its constraints

my love!
truth is in front of me, in my eyes
truth is in front of you, in your eyes
let nothing come in between
i and you, we and our love
and let us live life in love and passion
till we are here

Smruti Ranjan Mohanty

Sofia Skleida

Sofia Skleida was born in Athens. She is graduate of the Faculty of Filology at the National and Kapodistrian University of Athens. She has a MA in Pedagogy , a PhD in Comparative Pedagogy and she is also a postdoctoral candidate (Faculty of Theology, University of Athens). He has attended a number of training courses in special education and teaching, and especially in the teaching of literarure. He has also been trained and certified in Braille by the Center for Education and Rehabilitation of the Blind.

She published her first collection of poetry (Thessaloniki, 2014) entitled *Dream of Oasis*, which has been translated and published in Italy in 2017 (won the second prize in a international competition in Milan). A poem of the same collection became a song. Her first Fairy tale entitled *Geometrini* published in 2016 and her second fairy tale entitled *The Kingdom of Joy* was published in 2018.Recently were published her second and third collection of poetry entitled *Neologisms* and *Melismos* respectively. She is currently publishing two books titled *Cappadocian theological references in handwritten verses* and *The teaching of classical languages in the Italian secondary education.*She is a regular member at the Panhellenic Union of Writers.

Holy pilgrimage

Touching rare treasures

like that of your beauty

the look is enchanted by the ethos of your eyes

I feel the courage, I get your pulse

and I am losing with intensity on the beautiful seabed

The aroma of love is fragrant, sacred

as a rare relief, mosaic ...

Pantheon of wisdom

Full silence fits into the sense

of the divine existence

and the human presence

Where silently artistic

and imperial figures

of the past like Raphael,

inspiring the present

The dwelling of the Gods seeks the paternity

and the diffused light of the oculus

trigger memories ...

Playful time

I feel you…

palpating the yellow pages

of a forgotten book

struggling with many conflicting thoughts

I feel you ...

In the astigmatic memories of our fellow humans

in the silent voices of my desires

I'm nostalgic ...

Looking for the coveted redemption

Breathing the aroma of the hidden passion

Gripping the pulse

of my heartbeat ....

Remembering

our fallen soldiers of verse

Janet Perkins Caldwell

February 14, 1959 ~ September 20, 2016

Alan W. Jankowski

16 March 1961 ~ 10 March 2017

Coming
April 2020

The
World Healing, World Peace
International Poetry Symposium

Stay Tuned

for more information

intouch@innerchildpress.com

'building bridges of cultural understanding'

www.innerchildpress.com

Inner Child Press

News

Poetry Posse Members

We are so excited to share and announce a few of the current books, as well as the new and upcoming books of some of our Poetry Posse authors.

On the following pages we present to you ...

Jackie Davis Allen

Gail Weston Shazor

hülya n. yılmaz

Nizar Sartawi

Faleeha Hassan

Fahredin Shehu

Caroline 'Ceri' Nazareno

Eliza Segiet

William S. Peters, Sr.

Now Available at
www.innerchildpress.com

No Illusions

Through the Looking Glass

Jackie Davis Allen

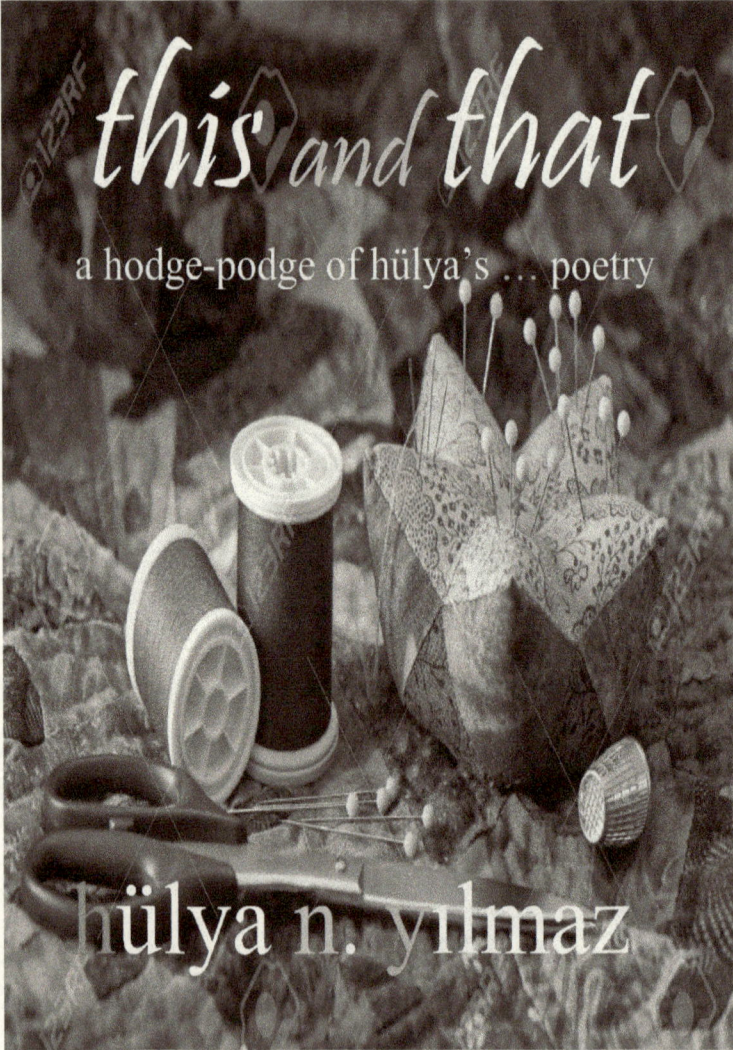
148

Now Available at
www.innerchildpress.com

Now Available at
www.innerchildpress.com

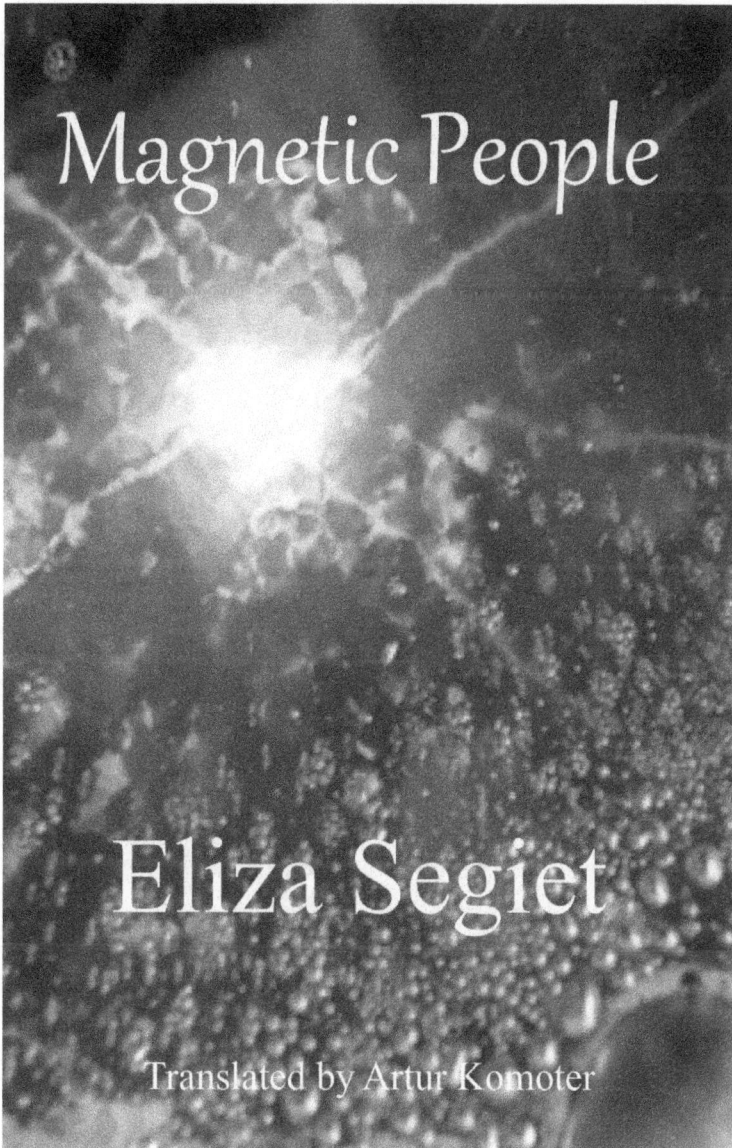

Magnetic People

Eliza Segiet

Translated by Artur Komoter

Dark Side
of the
Moon

Jackie Davis Allen

Now Available at
www.innerchildpress.com

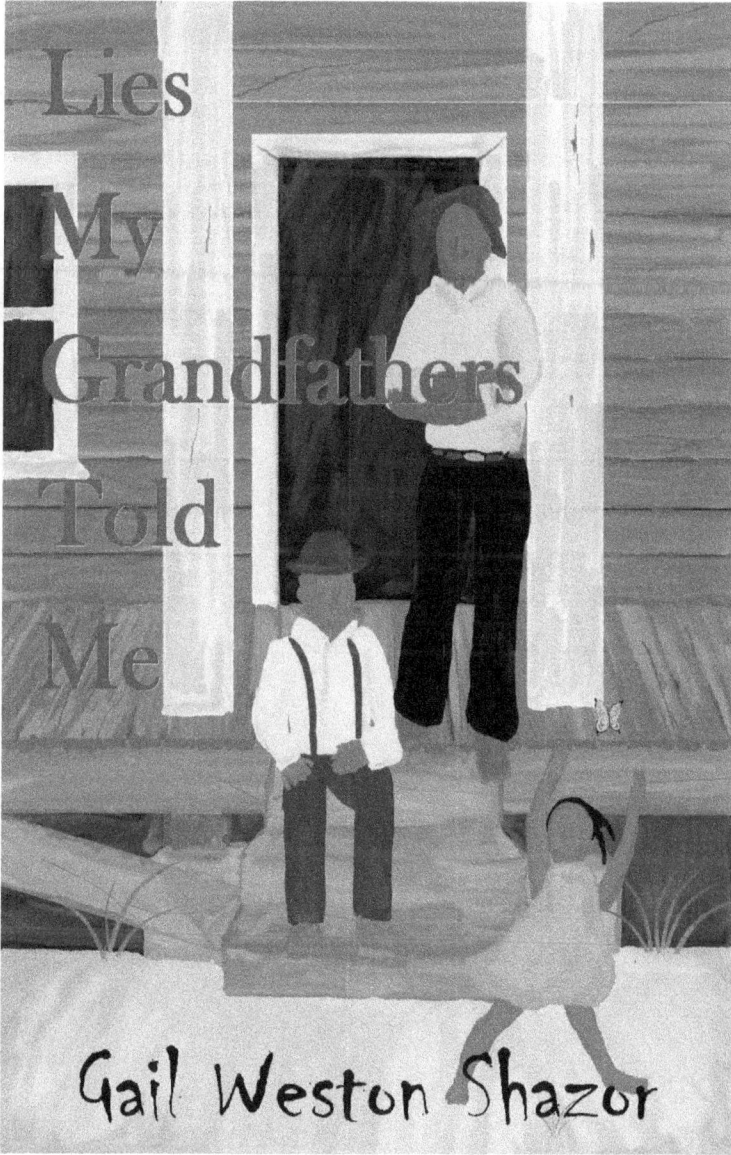

Lies My Grandfathers Told Me

Gail Weston Shazor

Now Available at
www.innerchildpress.com

Aflame

Memoirs in Verse

hülya n. yılmaz

Now Available at
www.innerchildpress.com

My Shadow

Nizar Sartawi

Inner Child Press News

Now Available at
www.innerchildpress.com

Mass Graves

Faleeha Hassan

Now Available at
www.innerchildpress.com

Breakfast

for

Butterflies

Faleeha Hassan

Inner Child Press News

Now Available at
www.innerchildpress.com

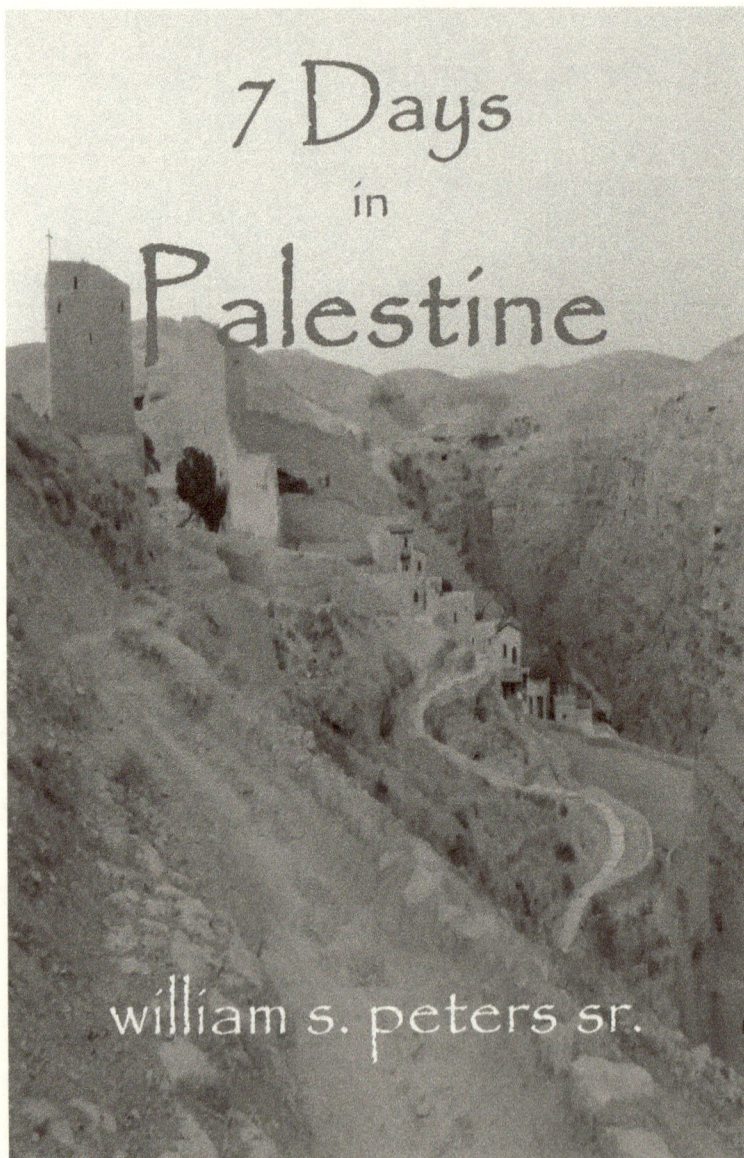

7 Days
in
Palestine

william s. peters sr.

Now Available at
www.innerchildpress.com

inner child press
presents

Tunisia My Love

william s. peters, sr.

Coming in the Summer of 2019

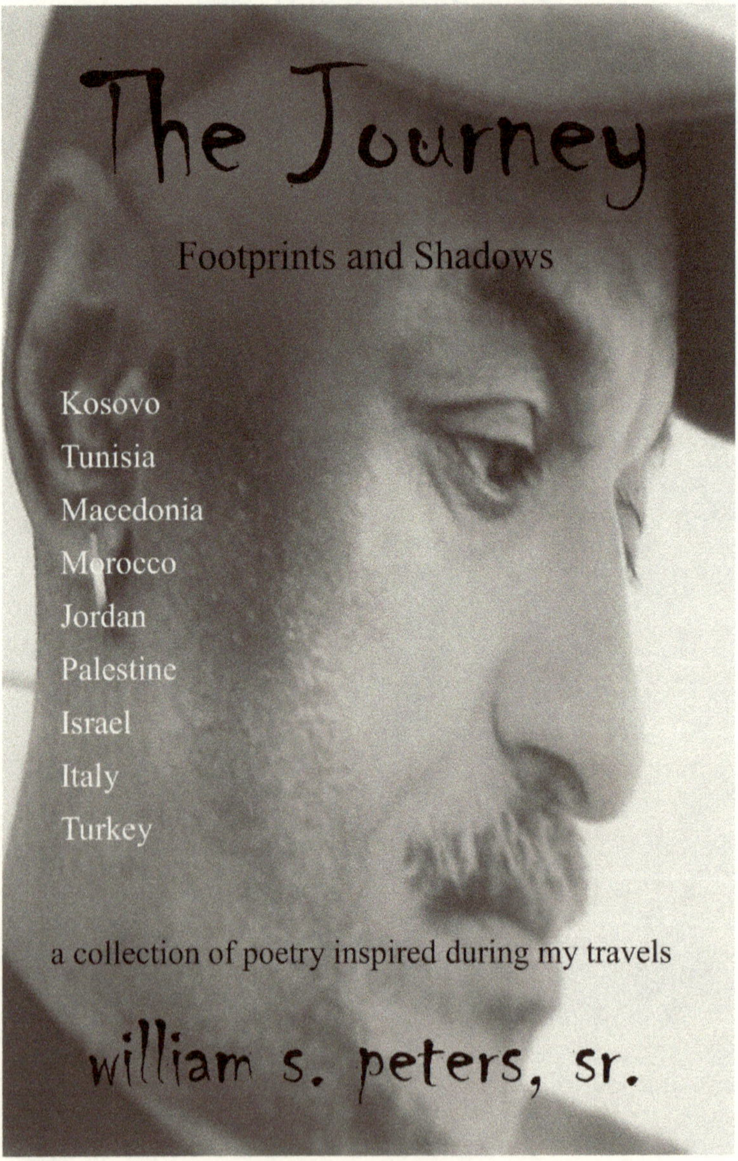

The Journey

Footprints and Shadows

Kosovo
Tunisia
Macedonia
Morocco
Jordan
Palestine
Israel
Italy
Turkey

a collection of poetry inspired during my travels

william s. peters, sr.

Now Available at
www.innerchildpress.com

Now Available at

www.innerchildpress.com

INNER CHILD PRESS

THIS IS WHY I
SLEEP

william s. peters sr.

Inward Reflections

Think on These Things
Book II

william s. peters, sr.

Now Available at
www.innerchildpress.com

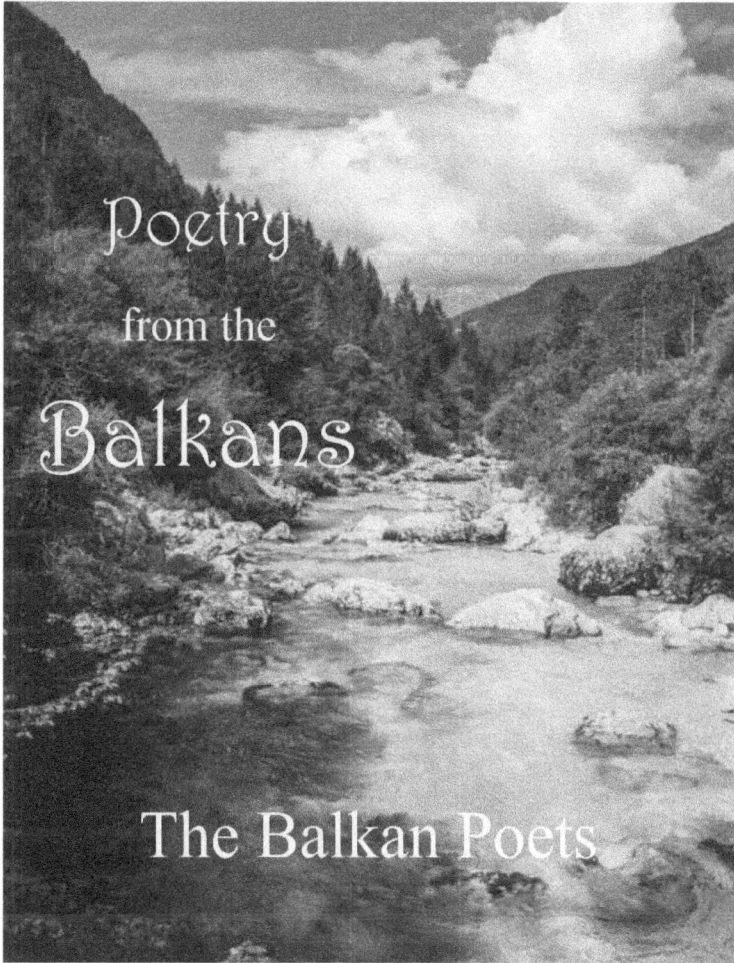

Poetry from the Balkans

The Balkan Poets

Other

Anthological

works from

Inner Child Press International

www.innerchildpress.com

Inner Child Press International
presents

A Love Anthology
2019

The Love Poets

Now Available

www.worldhealingworldpeacepoetry.com

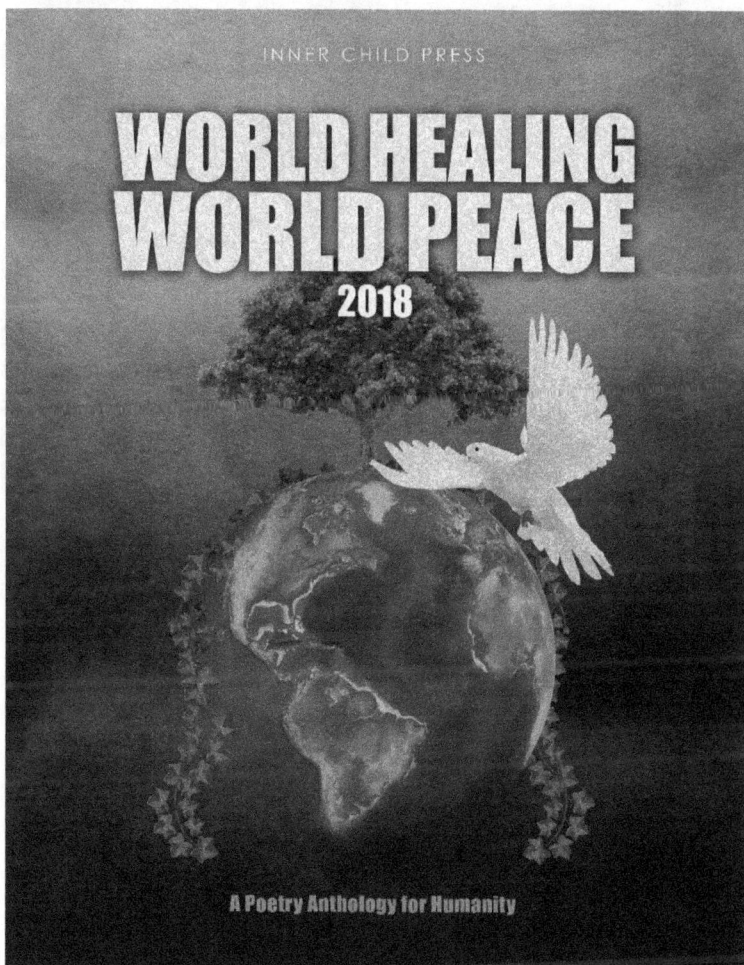

INNER CHILD PRESS

WORLD HEALING WORLD PEACE
2018

A Poetry Anthology for Humanity

Now Available

www.worldhealingworldpeacepoetry.com

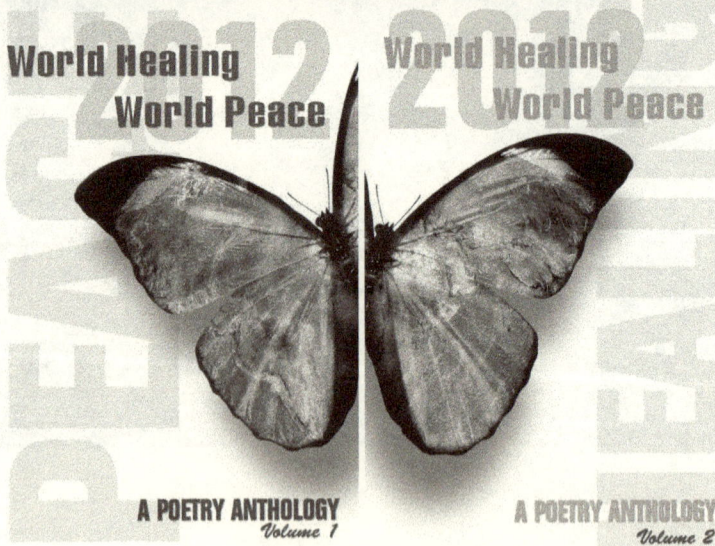

Now Available

www.worldhealingworldpeacepoetry.com

Now Available

Now Available

www.innerchildpress.com/anthologies

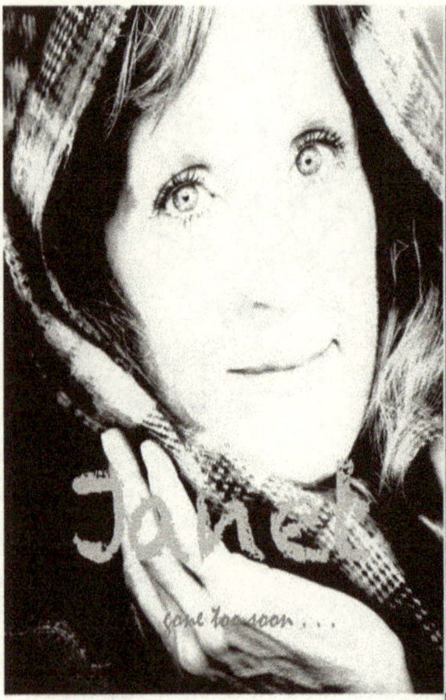

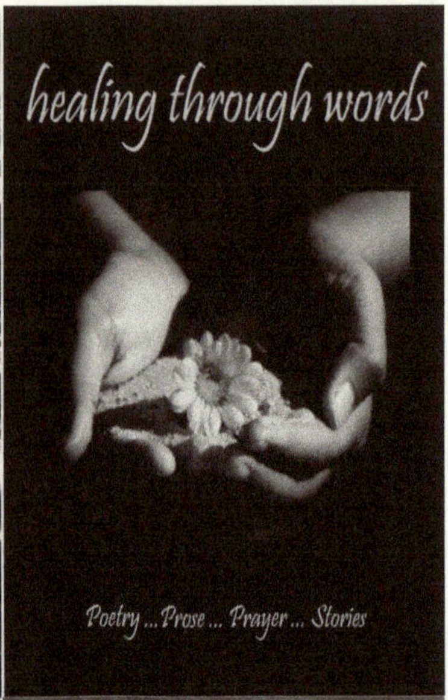

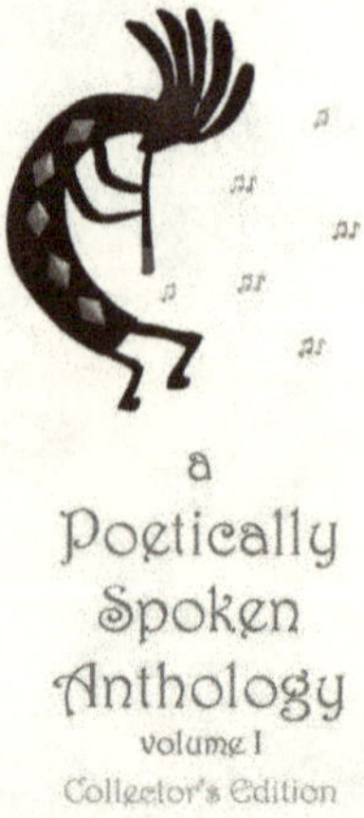

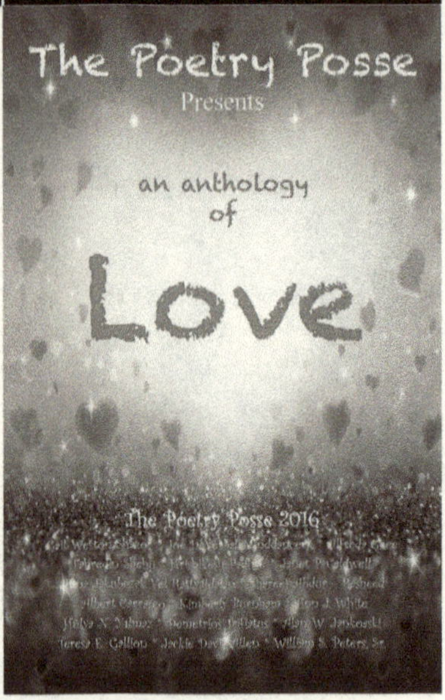

Now Available

www.innerchildpress.com/anthologies

Now Available

www.innerchildpress.com/anthologies

The Year of the Poet
January 2014

The Poetry Posse

Jamie Bond
Gail Weston Shazor
Albert 'Infinite' Carrasco
Siddartha Beth Pierce
Janet P. Caldwell
June 'Bugg' Barefield
Debbie M. Allen
Tony Henninger
Joe DaVerbal Minddancer
Robert Gibbons
Neetu Wali
Shareef Abdur-Rasheed
William S. Peters, Sr.

Carnation

Our January Feature
Terri L. Johnson

the Year of the Poet
February 2014

violets

The Poetry Posse

Jamie Bond
Gail Weston Shazor
Albert 'Infinite' Carrasco
Siddartha Beth Pierce
Janet P. Caldwell
June 'Bugg' Barefield
Debbie M. Allen
Tony Henninger
Joe DaVerbal Minddancer
Robert Gibbons
Neetu Wali
Shareef Abdur-Rasheed
William S. Peters, Sr.

Our February Features
Teresa E. Gallion & Robert Gibson

the Year of the Poet
March 2014

The Poetry Posse

Jamie Bond
Gail Weston Shazor
Albert 'Infinite' Carrasco
Siddartha Beth Pierce
Janet P. Caldwell
June 'Bugg' Barefield
Debbie M. Allen
Tony Henninger
Joe DaVerbal Minddancer
Robert Gibbons
Neetu Wali
Shareef Abdur-Rasheed
Kimberly Burnham
William S. Peters, Sr.

daffodil

Our March Featured Poets
AliciaC. Cooper & hülya yılmaz

the Year of the Poet
April 2014

The Poetry Posse

Jamie Bond
Gail Weston Shazor
Albert 'Infinite' Carrasco
Siddartha Beth Pierce
Janet P. Caldwell
June 'Bugg' Barefield
Debbie M. Allen
Tony Henninger
Joe DaVerbal Minddancer
Robert Gibbons
Neetu Wali
Shareef Abdur-Rasheed
Kimberly Burnham
William S. Peters, Sr.

Sweet Pea

Our April Featured Poets
Fahredin Shehu
Martina Reisz Newberry
Justin Blackburn
Monte Smith

celebrating international poetry month

Now Available

www.innerchildpress.com/the-year-of-the-poet

Now Available

www.innerchildpress.com/the-year-of-the-poet

The Year of the Poet
September 2014

Aster   **Morning-Glory**

Wild Child of September Birthday Flower

September Feature Poets
Florence Malone * Keith Alan Hamilton

The Poetry Posse
Jamie Bond * Gail Weston Shazor * Albert 'infinite' Carrasco * Siddartha Beth Pierce
Janet P. Caldwell * June 'Bugg' Barefield * Debbie M. Allen * Tony Henninger
Joe DaVerbal Minddancer * Robert Gibbons * Neetu Wali * Shareef Abdur-Rasheed
Kimberly Burnham * William S. Peters, Sr.

THE YEAR OF THE POET
October 2014

Red Poppy

The Poetry Posse
Jamie Bond * Gail Weston Shazor * Albert 'infinite' Carrasco * Siddartha Beth Pierce
Janet P. Caldwell * June 'Bugg' Barefield * Debbie M. Allen * Tony Henninger
Joe DaVerbal Minddancer * Robert Gibbons * Neetu Wali * Shareef Abdur-Rasheed
Kimberly Burnham * William S. Peters, Sr.

October Feature Poets
Ceri Naz * Rajendra Padhi * Elizabeth Castillo

THE YEAR OF THE POET
November 2014

Chrysanthemum

The Poetry Posse
Jamie Bond * Gail Weston Shazor * Albert 'infinite' Carrasco * Siddartha Beth Pierce
Janet P. Caldwell * June 'Bugg' Barefield * Debbie M. Allen * Tony Henninger
Joe DaVerbal Minddancer * Robert Gibbons * Neetu Wali * Shareef Abdur-Rasheed
Kimberly Burnham * William S. Peters, Sr.

November Feature Poets
Jocelyn Mosman * Jackie Allen * James Moore * Neville Hiatt

THE YEAR OF THE POET
December 2014

Narcissus

The Poetry Posse
Jamie Bond
Gail Weston Shazor
Albert 'infinite' Carrasco
Siddartha Beth Pierce
Janet P. Caldwell
June 'Bugg' Barefield
Debbie M. Allen
Tony Henninger
Joe DaVerbal Minddancer
Robert Gibbons
Neetu Wali
Shareef Abdur-Rasheed
Kimberly Burnham
William S. Peters, Sr.

December Feature Poets
Katherine Wyatt* WrittenInField * Santeo Lalpa * Justice Luke

Now Available

www.innerchildpress.com/the-year-of-the-poet

The Year of the Poet II
January 2015

Garnet

The Poetry Posse

Jamie Bond
Gail Weston Shazor
Albert 'Infinite' Carrasco
Siddartha Beth Pierce
Janet P. Caldwell
Tony Henninger
Joe DaVerbal Minddancer
Robert Gibbons
Neetu Wali
Shareef Abdur ~ Rasheed
Kimberly Burnham
Ann White
Keith Alan Hamilton
Katherine Wyatt
Fahredin Shehu
Hülya N. Yılmaz
Teresa E. Gallion
Jackie Allen
William S. Peters, Sr.

January Feature Poets
Bismay Mohanti * Jen Walls * Eric Judah

THE YEAR OF THE POET II
February 2015

Amethyst

THE POETRY POSSE

Jamie Bond
Gail Weston Shazor
Albert 'Infinite' Carrasco
Siddartha Beth Pierce
Janet P. Caldwell
Tony Henninger
Joe DaVerbal Minddancer
Robert Gibbons
Neetu Wali
Shareef Abdur ~ Rasheed
Kimberly Burnham
Ann White
Keith Alan Hamilton
Katherine Wyatt
Fahredin Shehu
Hülya N. Yılmaz
Teresa E. Gallion
Jackie Allen
William S. Peters, Sr.

FEBRUARY FEATURE POETS
Iram Fatima * Bob McNeil * Kerstin Centervall

The Year of the Poet II
March 2015

Our Featured Poets
Heung Sook * Anthony Arnold * Alicia Poland

Bloodstone

The Poetry Posse 2015
Jamie Bond * Gail Weston Shazor * Albert 'Infinite' Carrasco
Siddartha Beth Pierce * Janet P. Caldwell * Tony Henninger
Joe DaVerbal Minddancer * Neetu Wali * Shareef Abdur ~ Rasheed
Kimberly Burnham * Ann White * Keith Alan Hamilton
Katherine Wyatt * Fahredin Shehu * Hülya N. Yılmaz
Teresa E. Gallion * Jackie Allen * William S. Peters, Sr

The Year of the Poet II
April 2015

Celebrating International Poetry Month

Our Featured Poets
Raja Williams * Dennis Ferado * Laure Charazac

Diamonds

The Poetry Posse 2015
Jamie Bond * Gail Weston Shazor * Albert 'Infinite' Carrasco
Siddartha Beth Pierce * Janet P. Caldwell * Tony Henninger
Joe DaVerbal Minddancer * Neetu Wali * Shareef Abdur ~ Rasheed
Kimberly Burnham * Ann White * Keith Alan Hamilton
Katherine Wyatt * Fahredin Shehu * Hülya N. Yılmaz
Teresa E. Gallion * Jackie Allen * William S. Peters, Sr

Now Available

www.innerchildpress.com/the-year-of-the-poet

The Year of the Poet II
May 2015

May's Featured Poets
Geri Algeri
Akin Mosi Chinnery
Anna Jakubcza

Emeralds

The Poetry Posse 2015
Jamie Bond * Gail Weston Shazor * Albert 'Infinite' Carrasco
Siddartha Beth Pierce * Janet P. Caldwell * Tony Henninger
Joe DaVerbal Minddancer * Neetu Wali * Shareef Abdur – Rasheed
Kimberly Burnham * Ann White * Keith Alan Hamilton
Katherine Wyatt * Fahredin Shehu * Hülya N. Yılmaz
Teresa E. Gallion * Jackie Allen * William S. Peters, Sr.

The Year of the Poet II
June 2015

June's Featured Poets
Anahit Arustamyan * Yvette D. Murrell * Regina A. Walker

Pearl

The Poetry Posse 2015
Jamie Bond * Gail Weston Shazor * Albert 'Infinite' Carrasco
Siddartha Beth Pierce * Janet P. Caldwell * Tony Henninger
Joe DaVerbal Minddancer * Neetu Wali * Shareef Abdur – Rasheed
Kimberly Burnham * Ann White * Keith Alan Hamilton
Katherine Wyatt * Fahredin Shehu * Hülya N. Yılmaz
Teresa E. Gallion * Jackie Allen * William S. Peters, Sr.

The Year of the Poet II
July 2015

The Featured Poets for July 2015
Abhik Shome * Christina Neal * Robert Neal

Rubies

The Poetry Posse 2015
Jamie Bond * Gail Weston Shazor * Albert 'Infinite' Carrasco
Siddartha Beth Pierce * Janet P. Caldwell * Tony Henninger
Joe DaVerbal Minddancer * Neetu Wali * Shareef Abdur – Rasheed
Kimberly Burnham * Ann White * Keith Alan Hamilton
Katherine Wyatt * Fahredin Shehu * Hülya N. Yılmaz
Teresa E. Gallion * Jackie Allen * William S. Peters, Sr.

The Year of the Poet II
August 2015

Peridot

Featured Poets
Gayle Howell
Ann Chalasz
Christopher Schultz

The Poetry Posse 2015
Jamie Bond * Gail Weston Shazor * Albert 'Infinite' Carrasco
Siddartha Beth Pierce * Janet P. Caldwell * Tony Henninger
Joe DaVerbal Minddancer * Neetu Wali * Shareef Abdur – Rasheed
Kimberly Burnham * Ann White * Keith Alan Hamilton
Katherine Wyatt * Fahredin Shehu * Hülya N. Yılmaz
Teresa E. Gallion * Jackie Allen * William S. Peters, Sr.

Now Available

www.innerchildpress.com/the-year-of-the-poet

The Year of the Poet II
September 2015

Featured Poets

Alfreda Ghee   Lonneice Weeks Badley   Demetrios Trifiatis

Sapphires

The Poetry Posse 2015

Jamie Bond * Gail Weston Shazor * Albert 'Infinite' Carrasco
Siddartha Beth Pierce * Janet P. Caldwell * Tony Henninger
Joe DaVerbal Minddancer * Neetu Wali * Shareef Abdur – Rasheed
Kimberly Burnham * Ann White * Keith Alan Hamilton
Katherine Wyatt * Fahredin Shehu * Hülya N. Yılmaz
Teresa E. Gallion * Jackie Allen * William S. Peters, Sr.

The Year of the Poet II
October 2015

Featured Poets

Monte Smith * Laura J. Wolfe * William Washington

Opal

The Poetry Posse 2015

Jamie Bond * Gail Weston Shazor * Albert 'Infinite' Carrasco
Siddartha Beth Pierce * Janet P. Caldwell * Tony Henninger
Joe DaVerbal Minddancer * Neetu Wali * Shareef Abdur – Rasheed
Kimberly Burnham * Ann White * Keith Alan Hamilton
Katherine Wyatt * Fahredin Shehu * Hülya N. Yılmaz
Teresa E. Gallion * Jackie Allen * William S. Peters, Sr.

The Year of the Poet II
November 2015

Featured Poets
Alan W. Jankowski
Bismay Mohanty
James Moore

Topaz

The Poetry Posse 2015

Jamie Bond * Gail Weston Shazor * Albert 'Infinite' Carrasco
Siddartha Beth Pierce * Janet P. Caldwell * Tony Henninger
Joe DaVerbal Minddancer * Neetu Wali * Shareef Abdur – Rasheed
Kimberly Burnham * Ann White * Keith Alan Hamilton
Katherine Wyatt * Fahredin Shehu * Hülya N. Yılmaz
Teresa E. Gallion * Jackie Allen * William S. Peters, Sr.

The Year of the Poet II
December 2015

Featured Poets
Kerione Bryan * Michelle Joan Barulich * Neville Hiatt

Turquoise

The Poetry Posse 2015

Jamie Bond * Gail Weston Shazor * Albert 'Infinite' Carrasco
Siddartha Beth Pierce * Janet P. Caldwell * Tony Henninger
Joe DaVerbal Minddancer * Neetu Wali * Shareef Abdur – Rasheed
Kimberly Burnham * Ann White * Keith Alan Hamilton
Katherine Wyatt * Fahredin Shehu * Hülya N. Yılmaz
Teresa E. Gallion * Jackie Allen * William S. Peters, Sr.

Now Available

www.innerchildpress.com/the-year-of-the-poet

The Year of the Poet III
January 2016

Featured Poets

Lana Joseph * Atom Cyrus Rush * Christena Williams

Dark-eyed Junco

The Poetry Posse 2016

Gail Weston Shazor * Ilene Jakubczak Val Bytyshslena * Ann J. Wrico
Edwedin Shelat * Hrishikesh Padhye * Janet P. Caldwell
Joe DaVerbal Minddancer * Shareef Abdur - Rasheed
Albert Carrasco * Kimberly Burnham * Keith Alan Hamilton
Hulya N. Yılmaz * Demetrios Trifiatis * Alan W. Jankowski
Teresa E. Gallion * Jackie Davis Allen * William S. Peters, Sr.

The Year of the Poet III
February 2016

Featured Poets

Anthony Arnold
Anna Chalasz
Andre Rissambuga

Puffin

The Poetry Posse 2016

Gail Weston Shazor * Joe DaVerbal Minddancer * Alfreda Ghee
Edwedin Shelat * Hrishikesh Padhye * Janet P. Caldwell
Ilene Jakubczak Val Bytyshslena * Shareef Abdur - Rasheed
Albert Carrasco * Kimberly Burnham * Ann J. White
Hulya N. Yılmaz * Demetrios Trifiatis * Alan W. Jankowski
Teresa E. Gallion * Jackie Davis Allen * William S. Peters, Sr.

The Year of the Poet
March 2016

Featured Poets

Jeton Kelmendi   Nizar Sartawi   Sami Muhanna

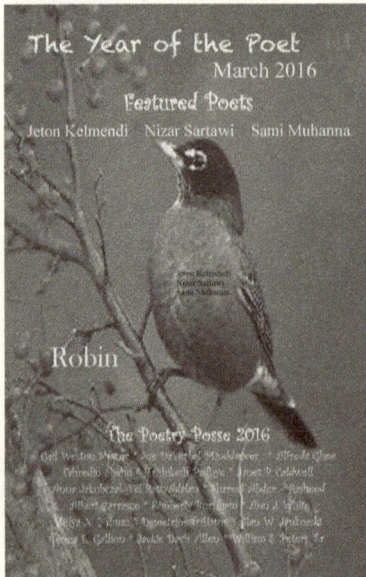

Robin

The Poetry Posse 2016

Gail Weston Shazor * Joe DaVerbal Minddancer * Alfreda Ghee
Edwedin Shelat * Hrishikesh Padhye * Janet P. Caldwell
Ilene Jakubczak Val Bytyshslena * Shareef Abdur - Rasheed
Albert Carrasco * Kimberly Burnham * Ann J. White
Hulya N. Yılmaz * Demetrios Trifiatis * Alan W. Jankowski
Teresa E. Gallion * Jackie Davis Allen * William S. Peters, Sr.

The Year of the Poet III

Featured Poets

Ali Abdolrezaei

Anna Chalasz

Agim Vinca

Ceri Naz

Black Capped Chickadee

The Poetry Posse 2016

Gail Weston Shazor * Joe DaVerbal Minddancer * Alfreda Ghee
Edwedin Shelat * Hrishikesh Padhye * Janet P. Caldwell
Anna Jakubczak Val Ban Adalin * Shareef Abdur - Rasheed
Albert Carrasco * Kimberly Burnham * Ann J. White
Hulya N. Yılmaz * Demetrios Trifiatis * Alan W. Jankowski
Teresa E. Gallion * Jackie Davis Allen * William S. Peters, Sr.

celebrating international poetry month

Now Available

www.innerchildpress.com/the-year-of-the-poet

The Year of the Poet
May 2016

Bob Strum
Barbara Allan
D.L. Davis

Oriole

The Poetry Posse 2016

The Year of the Poet III
June 2016

Featured Poets

Qibrije Demiri- Frangu
Naime Beqiraj
Faleeha Hassan
Bedri Zyberaj

Black Necked Stilt

The Poetry Posse 2016

The Year of the Poet II
July 2016

Iram Fatima 'Ashi
Langley Shazor
Jody Doty
Emilia T. Davis

Indigo Bunting

The Poetry Posse 2016

The Year of the Poet III
August 2016

Featured Poets

Anita Dash
Irena Jovanovic
Malgorzata Gouluda

Painted Bunting

The Poetry Posse 2016

Now Available

www.innerchildpress.com/the-year-of-the-poet

The Year of the Poet III
September 2016

Featured Poets

Simone Weber
Abhijit Sen
Eunice Barbara C. Novio

Long Billed Curle

The Poetry Posse 2016

The Year of the Poet III
October 2016

Featured Poets

Lana Joseph
Krishnamurthy
James Moore

The Poetry Posse 2016

The Year of the Poet III
November 2016

Featured Poets

Rosemary Burns
Robin Ouzman Hislop
Lonneice Weeks-Badley

Northern Cardinal

The Poetry Posse 2016

Gail Weston Shazor * Carolina Nazarian * Jen Walls
Nizar Sartawi * Janet P. Caldwell * Alfreda Ghee
Joe DaVerbal Minddancer * Shareef Abdur - Rasheed
Albert Carrasco * Kimberly Burnham * Elizabeth Castillo
Hülya N. Yılmaz * Demetrios Trifiatis * Alan W. Jankowski
Teresa E. Gallion * Jackie Davis Allen * William S. Peters, Sr.

The Year of the Poet III
December 2016

Featured Poets

Samih Masoud
Mountassir Aziz Bien
Abdulkadir Musa

Rough Legged Hawk

The Poetry Posse 2016

Now Available

www.innerchildpress.com/the-year-of-the-poet

The Year of the Poet IV
January 2017

Featur
Jon Winell
Natalie Shields
Iram Fatima "Ash"

Quaking Aspen

The Poetry Posse 2017

Gail Weston Shazor * Caroline Nazareno * Jhimay Mohanat
Nizar Sartawi * Anna Jakubczak Vel Ratty Adalan * Jen Walls
Joe DaVerbal Minddancer * Shareef Abdur - Rasheed
Albert Carrasco * Kimberly Burnham * Elizabeth Castillo
Hülya N. Yılmaz * Faleeha Hassan * Alan W. Jankowski
Teresa E. Gallion * Jackie Davis Allen * William S. Peters, Sr.

The Year of the Poet IV
February 2017

Featured Poets
Lin Ross
Soukaina Fathi
Anwer Ghani

Witch Hazel

The Poetry Posse 2017

Gail Weston Shazor * Caroline Nazareno * Jhimay Mohanat
Nizar Sartawi * Anna Jakubczak Vel Ratty Adalan * Jen Walls
Joe DaVerbal Minddancer * Shareef Abdur - Rasheed
Albert Carrasco * Kimberly Burnham * Elizabeth Castillo
Hülya N. Yılmaz * Faleeha Hassan * Alan W. Jankowski
Teresa E. Gallion * Jackie Davis Allen * William S. Peters, Sr.

The Year of the Poet IV
March 2017

Featured Poets
Tremell Stevens
Francisca Ricinski
Jamil Abu Shaih

The Eastern Redbud

The Poetry Posse 2017

Gail Weston Shazor * Caroline Nazareno * Jhimay Mohanat
Teresa E. Gallion * Anna Jakubczak Vel Ratty Adalan
Joe DaVerbal Minddancer * Shareef Abdur - Rasheed
Albert Carrasco * Kimberly Burnham * Elizabeth Castillo
Hülya N. Yılmaz * Faleeha Hassan * Jackie Davis Allen
Jen Walls * Nizar Sartawi * * William S. Peters, Sr.

The Year of the Poet IV
April 2017

Featured Poets
Dr. Ruchida Barman
Neptune Barman
Masood Khalaf

The Blossoming Cherry

The Poetry Posse 2017

Gail Weston Shazor * Caroline Nazareno * Jhimay Mohanat
Teresa E. Gallion * Anna Jakubczak Vel Ratty Adalan
Joe DaVerbal Minddancer * Shareef Abdur - Rasheed
Albert Carrasco * Kimberly Burnham * Elizabeth Castillo
Hülya N. Yılmaz * Faleeha Hassan * Jackie Davis Allen
Jen Walls * Nizar Sartawi * * William S. Peters, Sr.

Now Available

www.innerchildpress.com/the-year-of-the-poet

The Year of the Poet IV
May 2017

The Flowering Dogwood Tree

Featured Poets
Kallisa Powell
Alicja Maria Kuberska
Fethi Sassi

The Poetry Posse 2017

Gail Weston Shazor * Caroline Nazareno * Jhimmy Mohanty
Teresa E. Gallion * Anna Jakubczak Vel Ratty Adalan
Joe DaVerbal Minddancer * Shareef Abdur – Rasheed
Albert Carrasco * Kimberly Burnham * Elizabeth Castillo
Hülya N. Yılmaz * Teledia Hassan * Jackie Davis Allen
Jen Walls * Nizar Sartawi * * William S. Peters, Sr.

The Year of the Poet IV
June 2017

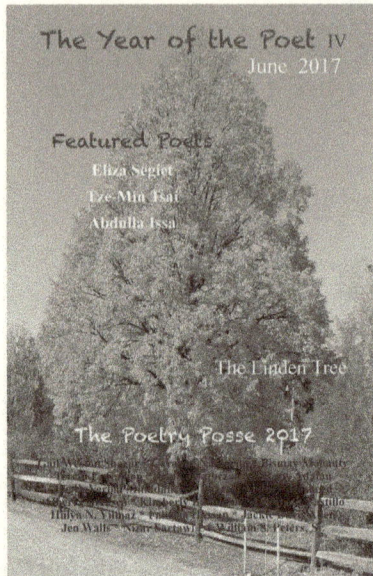

Featured Poets
Eliza Segiet
Eze-Mia Tsai
Abdulla Issa

The Linden Tree

The Poetry Posse 2017

Jhimmy Mohanty

Hülya N. Yılmaz *
Jen Walls * Nizar Sartawi * William S. Peters,

The Year of the Poet IV
July 2017

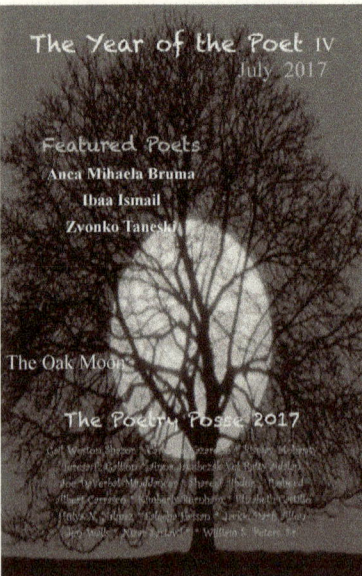

Featured Poets
Anca Mihaela Bruma
Ibaa Ismail
Zvonko Taneski

The Oak Moon

The Poetry Posse 2017

Gail Weston Shazor * Caroline Nazareno * Jhimmy Mohanty
Teresa E. Gallion * Anna Jakubczak Vel Ratty Adalan
Joe DaVerbal Minddancer * Shareef Abdur – Rasheed
Albert Carrasco * Kimberly Burnham * Elizabeth Castillo
Hülya N. Yılmaz * Teledia Hassan * Jackie Davis Allen
Jen Walls * Nizar Sartawi * * William S. Peters, Sr.

The Year of the Poet IV
August 2017

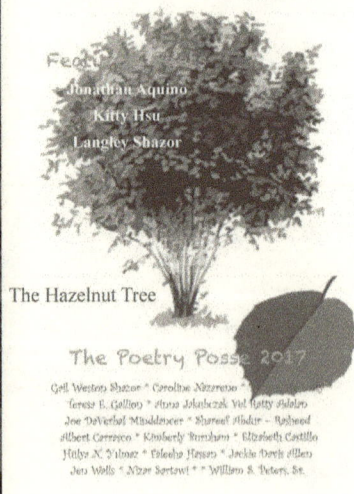

Featured Poets
Jonathan Aquino
Kitty Hsu
Langley Shazor

The Hazelnut Tree

The Poetry Posse 2017

Gail Weston Shazor * Caroline Nazareno *
Teresa E. Gallion * Anna Jakubczak Vel Ratty Adalan
Joe DaVerbal Minddancer * Shareef Abdur – Rasheed
Albert Carrasco * Kimberly Burnham * Elizabeth Castillo
Hülya N. Yılmaz * Teledia Hassan * Jackie Davis Allen
Jen Walls * Nizar Sartawi * * William S. Peters, Sr.

Now Available

www.innerchildpress.com/the-year-of-the-poet

The Year of the Poet IV
September 2017

Featured Poets

Martina Reisz Newberry
Ameer Nassir
Christine Fulco Neal
Robert Neal

The Elm Tree

The Poetry Posse 2017

Gail Weston Shazor * Caroline Nazareno * Bismay Mohanty
Teresa E. Gallion * Anna Jakubczak Vel Ratty Adalan
Joe DaVerbal Minddancer * Shareef Abdur – Rasheed
Albert Carrasco * Kimberly Burnham * Elizabeth Castillo
Hülya N. Yılmaz * Faleeha Hassan * Jackie Davis Allen
Jen Walls * Nizar Sartawi * * William S. Peters, Sr.

The Year of the Poet IV
October 2017

Featured Poets

Ahmed Abu Saleem
Nedal Al-Qaeim
Sadeddin Shahin

The Black Walnut Tree

The Poetry Posse 2017

Gail Weston Shazor * Caroline Nazareno * Bismay Mohanty
Teresa E. Gallion * Anna Jakubczak Vel Ratty Adalan
Joe DaVerbal Minddancer * Shareef Abdur – Rasheed
Albert Carrasco * Kimberly Burnham * Elizabeth Castillo
Hülya N. Yılmaz * Faleeha Hassan * Jackie Davis Allen
Jen Walls * Nizar Sartawi * * William S. Peters, Sr.

The Year of the Poet IV
November 2017

Featured Poets

Kay Peters
Alfreda D. Ghee
Gabriella Garofalo
Rosemary Cappello

The Tree of Life

The Poetry Posse 2017

Gail Weston Shazor * Caroline Nazareno * Bismay Mohanty
Teresa E. Gallion * Anna Jakubczak Vel Ratty Adalan
Joe DaVerbal Minddancer * Shareef Abdur – Rasheed
Albert Carrasco * Kimberly Burnham * Elizabeth Castillo
Hülya N. Yılmaz * Faleeha Hassan * Jackie Davis Allen
Jen Walls * Nizar Sartawi * William S. Peters, Sr.

The Year of the Poet IV
December 2017

Featured Poets

Justice Clarke
Mariel M. Pabroa
Kiley Brown

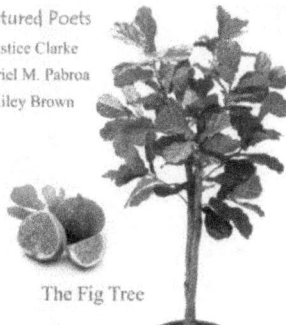

The Fig Tree

The Poetry Posse 2017

Gail Weston Shazor * Caroline Nazareno * Bismay Mohanty
Teresa E. Gallion * Anna Jakubczak Vel Ratty Adalan
Joe DaVerbal Minddancer * Shareef Abdur – Rasheed
Albert Carrasco * Kimberly Burnham * Elizabeth Castillo
Hülya N. Yılmaz * Faleeha Hassan * Jackie Davis Allen
Jen Walls * Nizar Sartawi * William S. Peters, Sr.

Now Available

www.innerchildpress.com/the-year-of-the-poet

Inner Child Press Anthologies

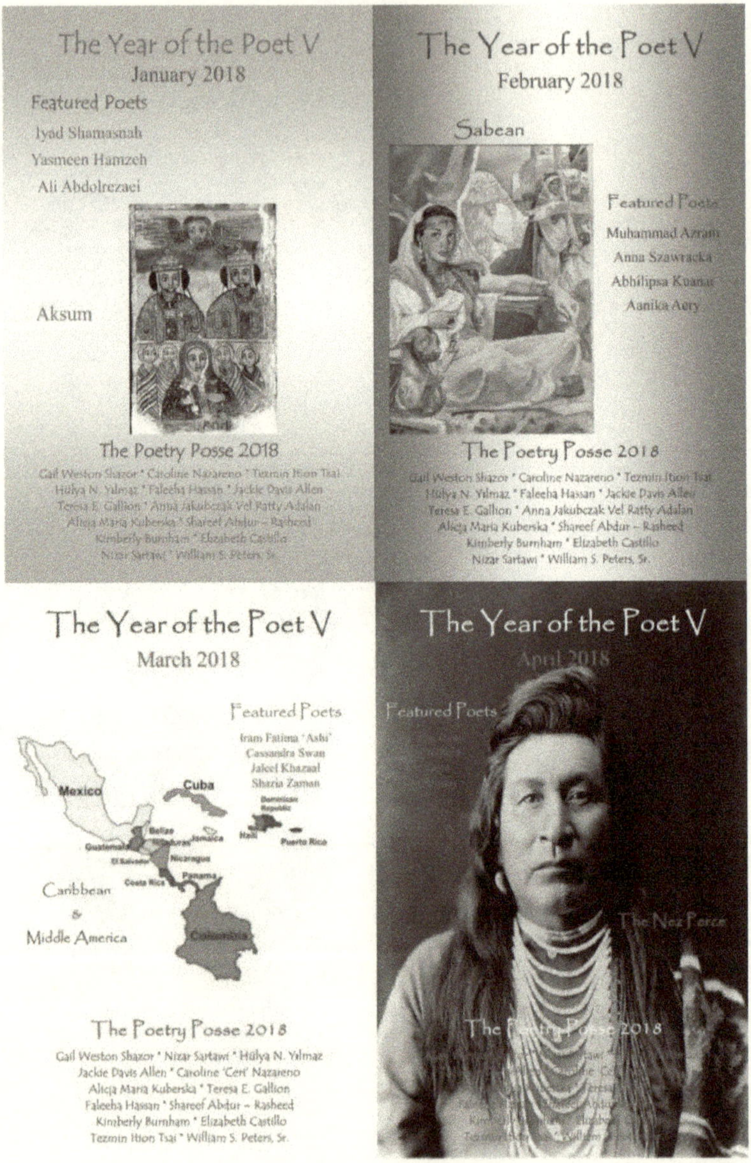

Now Available

www.innerchildpress.com/the-year-of-the-poet

The Year of the Poet V
May 2018

Featured Poets
Zaldy Campos de León, Jr
Sybela K. Malinowska
Emilio Ahmed
Ofelia Pisdan

The Sumerians

The Poetry Posse 2018
Gail Weston Shazor * Nizar Sartawi * Hülya N. Yılmaz
Jackie Davis Allen * Caroline 'Ceri' Nazareno
Alicja Maria Kuberska * Teresa E. Gallion
Kimberly Burnham * Shareef Abdur – Rasheed
Faleeha Hassan * Elizabeth Castillo * Swapna Behera
Tezmin Ition Tsai * William S. Peters, Sr.

The Year of the Poet V
June 2018

Featured Poets
Bilall Maloqi * Daim Mihari * Gojko Božović * Sofija Živković

The Paleo Indians

The Poetry Posse 2018

The Year of the Poet V
July 2018

Featured Poets

Oceania

The Poetry Posse 2018

The Year of the Poet V
August 2018

Featured Poets
Hussein Habasch * Mircea Dan Duta * Naida Mujkić * Swagat Das

The Lapita

The Poetry Posse 2018
Gail Weston Shazor * Nizar Sartawi * Hülya N. Yılmaz
Jackie Davis Allen * Caroline 'Ceri' Nazareno
Alicja Maria Kuberska * Teresa E. Gallion
Kimberly Burnham * Shareef Abdur – Rasheed
Ashok K. Bhargava* Elizabeth Castillo * Swapna Behaera
Tezmin Ition Tsai * William S. Peters, Sr.

Now Available

www.innerchildpress.com/the-year-of-the-poet

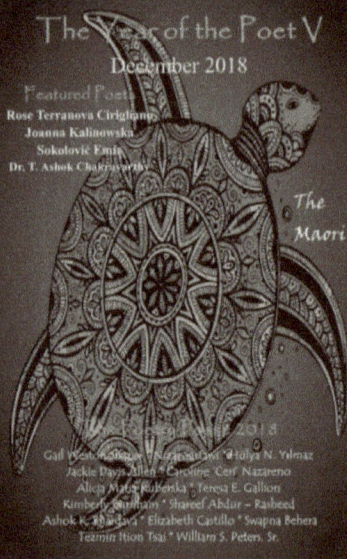

190

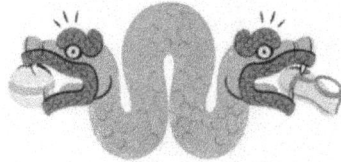

The Year of the Poet VI
May 2019

Featured Poets

Emad Al-Haydary * Hussein Nasser Jabr
Wahab Sheriff * Abdul Razzaq Al Ameeri

Asia Southeast Asia and Maritime Asia

The Poetry Posse 2019

Gail Weston Shazor * Albert Carrasco * Hülya N. Yılmaz
Jackie Davis Allen * Caroline Nazareno * Eliza Segiet
Alicja Maria Kubersla * Teresa E. Gallion * Joe Paire
Kimberly Burnham * Shareef Abdur – Rasheed
Ashok K. Bhargava * Elizabeth Castillo * Swapna Behera
Tezmin Ition Tsai * William S. Peters, Sr.

The Year of the Poet VI
June 2019

Featured Poets

Kate Gaudi Powiekszone * Sahaj Sabharwal
Iwu Jeff * Mohamed Abdel Aziz Shmeis

Arctic
Circumpolar

The Poetry Posse 2019

Gail Weston Shazor * Albert Carrasco * Hülya N. Yılmaz
Jackie Davis Allen * Caroline Nazareno * Eliza Segiet
Alicja Maria Kubersla * Teresa E. Gallion * Joe Paire
Kimberly Burnham * Shareef Abdur – Rasheed
Ashok K. Bhargava * Elizabeth Castillo * Swapna Behera
Tezmin Ition Tsai * William S. Peters, Sr.

The Year of the Poet VI
July 2019

Featured Poets

Siradeddin Shahin   Andy Scott
Fahredin Shehu   Alok Kumar Ray

The Horn of Africa

Ethiopia   Djibouti

Somalia   Eritrea

The Poetry Posse 2019

Gail Weston Shazor * Albert Carrasco * Hülya N. Yılmaz
Jackie Davis Allen * Caroline Nazareno * Eliza Segiet
Alicja Maria Kubersla * Teresa E. Gallion * Joe Paire
Kimberly Burnham * Shareef Abdur – Rasheed
Ashok K. Bhargava * Elizabeth Castillo * Swapna Behera
Tezmin Ition Tsai * William S. Peters, Sr.

The Year of the Poet VI
August 2019

Featured Poets

Shola Balogun * Bharati Nayak
Monalisa Dash Dwibedy * Mbizo Chirasha

Coexist

Southwest Asia

The Poetry Posse 2019

Gail Weston Shazor * Albert Carrasco * Hülya N. Yılmaz
Jackie Davis Allen * Caroline Nazareno * Eliza Segiet
Alicja Maria Kubersla * Teresa E. Gallion * Joe Paire
Kimberly Burnham * Shareef Abdur – Rasheed
Ashok K. Bhargava * Elizabeth Castillo * Swapna Behera
Tezmin Ition Tsai * William S. Peters, Sr.

Now Available

www.innerchildpress.com/the-year-of-the-poet

The Year of the Poet VI
September 2019

Featured Poets

Elena Liliana Popescu * Gobinda Biswas
Iram Fatima 'Ashi' * Joseph S. Spence, Sr.

The Caucasus

The Poetry Posse 2019

Gail Weston Shazor * Albert Carrasco * Hülya N. Yılmaz
Jackie Davis Allen * Caroline Nazareno * Eliza Segiet
Alicja Maria Kuberska * Teresa E. Gallion * Joe Paire
Kimberly Burnham * Shareef Abdur – Rasheed
Ashok K. Bhargava * Elizabeth Castillo * Swapna Behera
Tezmin Ition Tsai * William S. Peters, Sr.

The Year of the Poet VI
October 2019

Featured Poets

Ngozi Olivia Osuoha * Denisa Kondić
Pankhuri Sinha * Christena AV Williams

The Nile Valley

The Poetry Posse 2019

Gail Weston Shazor * Albert Carrasco * Hülya N. Yılmaz
Jackie Davis Allen * Caroline Nazareno * Eliza Segiet
Alicja Maria Kuberska * Teresa E. Gallion * Joe Paire
Kimberly Burnham * Shareef Abdur – Rasheed
Ashok K. Bhargava * Elizabeth Castillo * Swapna Behera
Tezmin Ition Tsai * William S. Peters, Sr.

The Year of the Poet VI
November 2019

Featured Poets

Rozalia Aleksandrova * Orbindu Ganga
Smruti Ranjan Mohanty * Sofia Skleida

Northern Asia

The Poetry Posse 2019

Gail Weston Shazor * Albert Carrasco * Hülya N. Yılmaz
Jackie Davis Allen * Caroline Nazareno * Eliza Segiet
Alicja Maria Kuberska * Teresa E. Gallion * Joe Paire
Kimberly Burnham * Shareef Abdur – Rasheed
Ashok K. Bhargava * Elizabeth Castillo * Swapna Behera
Tezmin Ition Tsai * William S. Peters, Sr.

Now Available

www.innerchildpress.com/the-year-of-the-poet

and there is much, much more !

visit . . .

www.innerchildpress.com/antho
logies-sales-special.php

Also check out our Authors and
all the wonderful Books
Available at :

www.innerchildpress.com/autho
rs-pages

INNER CHILD PRESS

WORLD HEALING WORLD PEACE
2018

A Poetry Anthology for Humanity

Now Available

www.worldhealingworldpeacepoetry.com

Now Available

I Support

World Healing
World Peace

www.worldhealingworldpeacepoetry.com

197

World Healing
World Peace
2018

Now Available

www.worldhealingworldpeacepoetry.com

Inner Child Press International

'building bridges of cultural understanding'

Meet our Cultural Ambassadors

Fahredin Shehu
Director of Cultural

Faleha Hassan
Iraq – USA

Elizabeth E. Castillo
Philippines

Antoinette Coleman
Chicago
Midwest USA

Ananda Nepali
Nepal – Tibet
Northern India

Kimberly Burnham
Pacific Northwest
USA

Alicja Kuberska
Poland
Eastern Europe

Swapna Behera
India
Southeast Asia

Kolade O. Freedom
Nigeria
West Africa

Monsif Beroual
Morocco
Northern Africa

Ashok K. Bhargava
Canada

Tzemin Ition Tsai
Republic of China
Greater China

Alicia M. Ramirez
Mexico
Central America

Christena AV Williams
Jamaica
Caribbean

Louise Hudon
Eastern Canada

Aziz Mountassir
Morocco
Northern Africa

Shareef Abdur-Rasheed
Southeastern USA

Laure Charazac
France
Western Europe

Mohammad Ikbal Harb
Lebanon
Middle East

**Mohamed Abdel
Aziz Shmeis**
Egypt
Middle East

Hilary Mainga
Kenya
Eastern Africa

Josephus R. Johnson
Liberia

www.innerchildpress.com

200

This Anthological Publication
is underwritten solely by

Inner Child Press

Inner Child Press is a Publishing Company Founded and Operated by Writers. Our personal publishing experiences provides us an intimate understanding of the sometimes daunting challenges Writers, New and Seasoned may face in the Business of Publishing and Marketing their Creative "Written Work".

For more Information

Inner Child Press

www.innerchildpress.com

Inner Child Press International

'building bridges of cultural understanding'

202 Wiltree Court, State College, Pennsylvania 16801

www.innerchildpress.com

~ fini ~